THE FIRST GUN SHOTS OF THE GREAT WAR

HULL MEN AT THE FRONT IN 1914-15

Dedication

To those Hull men serving at the front on land and sea in 1914-15 and over 1,200 who lost their lives before conscription.

Contents

	Acknowledgements	v
	Picture Credits	vi
	Terms and Abbreviations	vii
	Foreword	viii
	Introduction	ix
Chapter 1	The Checks and Balances Break Down Across Europe	1
Chapter 2	Scarlet Tunics and Bearskins; Hull Coldstreamers in 1914	7
Chapter 3	Deadlock at the Aisne; The 1st East Yorks Arrive at the Aisne	35
Chapter 4	Taking the King's Shilling; Hull Volunteers in 1914	45
Chapter 5	Please Come Quickly! The East Yorkshire Regiment at Second Ypres	65
Chapter 6	Distant Guns; The 6th East Yorks sail For Gallipoli	85
Chapter 7	You're Needed Now! Conscription Looms	105
Chapter 8	What became of the men of 1914-15?	109
	Conclusion	121
	Appendix	123
	Index	137

First Published 2015

By Simon Dinsdale
East Riding of Yorkshire

Printed and Bound in Great Britain by
The Amadeus Press
Ezra House
West 26 Business Park
Cleckheaton
BD19 4TQ

ISBN: 978-0-9933875-0-0

All rights reserved. No part of this publication may be reproduced, in any shape or form or by any means electronicalm, digital, mechanical, photographic, photocopied or stored in any retrieval system without prior written permission of Simon Dinsdale.

© Simon Dinsdale
Copy Right to this Document belongs to the Author Simon Dinsdale

Acknowledgements

To all those who have helped or encouraged me to put this publication together over the past two years, listed in alphabetical order a big thank you to all.

Special thanks to Military Historian and prolific author B.S Barnes for writing the Foreword and casting his expert eye over my manuscript before going to print. Barrie has done more than anyone in this region during the past twenty years to bring to our attention the experiences and sacrifices of East Yorkshire men in the two world wars through several publications. I first read This Righteous War twenty five years ago and it has travelled with me to five different houses during that time. The book tells of the experiences of the Hull (Pals) 92nd Brigade in the Great War, years before anybody else had written on the subject.

I am very grateful to Kath Burrows for the laborious but very important and responsible task of proof reading this book before going to print.

The staff of the Hull History Centre for their help and assistance over the past two years and Lizzy Baker, Senior Public Services Officer, and her staff at the East Riding of Yorkshire Archives and Local Studies Centre Beverley .

For the information on his great uncle Harry Rands Parrott of the 1st East Yorkshire Regiment thank you to Bernard Hill.

In 1989 Malcolm and Mary Mann compiled an index of local individuals and events relating to the Great War sourced from the Hull Daily Mail. It is a very useful source and index for historians or anyone looking for family members who have appeared in the newspaper during the war and must have taken thousands of hours to complete. It is available to all at the Hull History Centre and is an excellent reference guide.

Local firm Sandersons Solicitors 19 Parliament Street Hull and Michael Reed the company's archivist kindly gave me his time and allowed me access to their records regarding employees who enlisted in 1914.

Andrew Robinson of the Yorkshire Post for featuring my research on the Tock family on 4th August 2014 the centenary of the outbreak of the Great War.

Karen Tomlinson for her support and help with all things IT, and my brother Marcos who has helped to enhance some of the images which appear here.

The Tock family and in particular David the last surviving son of Stanley Tock 6th East Yorkshire Regiment who was one of ten brothers who would all see service in the army and navy during the war. I have had the pleasure of meeting with David on several occasions for the odd pint and he has shared with me some of his family's wartime experiences, including several photographs some of which appear here.

ITV Reporter James Webster for his interest in my research.

Picture Credits

Many of the photos of local men come from the Hull Daily Mail, Hull Daily News, and the Hull & Lincolnshire Times 1914-1916.

Thank you to the following individuals and organisations.

Nigel Waller for his excellent photography which include Hull Cenotaph, The former Hull Police Station, Parliament Street, Memorial plaques Richard Erle Benson, and Osborn Cecil Wilkinson, East Yorkshire Regiment Beverley Minister.

The Slack Family/.eastriding.net (Cecil Moorhouse Slack East Yorkshire Regiment).

David Tock Family Collection, (Stanley Tock, 6th East Yorkshire Regiment).

Patricia Wilkinson Family Collection, (Reginald Anthony, Sandersons Solicitors, East Yorkshire Regiment).

The National Portrait Gallery London,(Lieutenant Colonel Walter Herbert Young East Yorkshire Regiment by Lafayette 1931).

Military Terms and Abbreviations

ANZAC	Australian & New Zealand Army Corps
BEF	British Expeditionary Force
CO	Commanding Officer
CPL	Corporal
DCM	Distinguished Conduct Medal
DSO	Distinguished Service Order
EYR	East Yorkshire Regiment
KOYLI	Kings Own Yorkshire Light Infantry
MiD	Mentioned in Despatches
MO	Medical Officer
NCO	Non Commissioned Officer
NER	North Eastern Railway
OC	Officer Commanding
OLD CONTEMPTIBLE	A Soldier serving in France/Belgium August-December 1914
OTC	Officer Training Corps
P.C	Police Constable
PTE	Junior Soldier belonging to an Infantry Regiment
RAMC	Royal Army Medical Corps
RESERVIST	Former serviceman eligible for further military service
R.H.A	Royal Horse Artillery
R.F.A	Royal Field Artillery
RE	Royal Engineers
V.A.D	Voluntary Aid Detachment
WYR	West Yorkshire Regiment

Foreword

B.S Barnes

Military Historian

This study tells the story of men from the City of Hull who served in the army, navy, and Merchant Navy in the first 16 months of The Great War August 1914-December 1915. In this pre-conscription Era all of Britain's Armed Forces consisted of Volunteers. This is one period of Hull's history that has been neglected by historians and by covering this period, Simon has produced a volume that will be essential reading for any student of the history of Hull and The Great War. His enthusiasm for the subject shines through on every page. He sets the scene admirably before introducing us to the individual characters from Hull, my home city. The photographs of these people give added poignancy to their tragic deaths in Belgium, France, and Gallipoli. The result of Simon's hard work is an excellent piece of research and a fascinating book.

Every Remembrance Sunday the Faithful gather to echo these immortal lines, "We shall remember them" but in truth it gets harder and harder to do so with every passing generation. In producing this volume the author gives us a much clearer picture of those we remember and of the price paid by that great city during that time. Within these pages they live again.

I congratulate Simon on his persistence and diligence which has led to the publication of this important and informative volume and I highly recommend it to anyone, like myself, with an interest in the City of Hull and its military traditions.

B.S Barnes May 2015

Introduction

Britain, unlike her European neighbours, did not compel men to serve in the military and had a small but highly professional army in 1914, compared to the huge standing armies of France, Russia and Germany, where national service for conscripts had been increased from two to three years. Britain's ultimatum to Germany expired on a Tuesday evening at 11.00pm 4th August 1914 (Midnight European time). During the following day, all British regiments had received their mobilisation orders, whilst thousands of army and navy Reservists were instructed to present themselves at numerous military barracks across the country. The British Army of the First World War is by far the largest this nation has ever raised and whilst estimates do vary, a figure of 5.7 million is widely accepted but in 1914, less than 350,000 men from Britain and her Empire served in France and Belgium, suffering casualties of around 90,000. Some 75,000 Hull men were involved on all fronts from August 1914 until the final days of November 1918 but it is those local men at war in the early months and years of 1914-15 that I am concerned with here, before the Military Service Act of January 1916 compelled men aged between 18 and 41 to join one branch of the Military. The local men who saw military action in 1914 were all currently serving with the army and navy or Reservists called back to the colours, ensuring Hull fatalities were relatively light compared to future years (around 225 by the end of 1914). By the 6th August there were over 100 local men amongst the ranks of the two Guards brigades with many involved in the exhausting retreat from Mons just three weeks later. The 1st East Yorkshire Regiment would embark for France in September and suffer hundreds of casualties by December with more Hull men being killed in 1914 serving with the regiment than any other. The 4th East Yorkshire Regiment, a Territorial battalion, left for France in April 1915 with several of Hull's leading businessmen serving as senior officers, whilst the 6th East Yorkshire Regiment raised at Beverley in 1914 as part of Kitchener's New Armies, would be serving thousands of miles away in the Dardanelles by August 1915.

Hull's maritime industry ensured many local fishermen were immediately recruited to serve aboard armed trawlers and minesweepers often involved in hazardous operations off the Yorkshire Coast and the North Sea from the outset of the conflict. Thomas Jackson may have been Hull's first fisherman to lose his life when the Hull trawler Imperialist hit a mine on 10th September 1914. Stoker Walker and William Fagg were two Hull men serving aboard the 'HMS Aboukir', one of three obsolete British cruisers sunk in September 1914 with the loss of over 1,400 men. Of the 7,000 Hull men who would lose their lives during the war around 17 per cent were seamen, accounting for around 1,200 lives.

The call to arms was sudden and life changing, with men having to leave their families and walk out of jobs which they had occupied for years to report to

Gunner James Sharpe wounded at Mons on Sunday 23rd August

barracks the length and breadth of the country within 48 hours. It is difficult to think of an area across the country that was as suddenly and directly affected as the Yorkshire Wolds, with the immediate loss of hundreds of skilled rural workers. They had joined the Waggoners Special Reserve formed at Sledmere in 1912 and were called up en masse at the outbreak of war. These men were not former servicemen but civilians who were part of a Special Transport Reserve. They received their call up papers at remote farms spread across the rugged Yorkshire Wolds whilst the harvest was in full swing. By 6th August they were all gone with farriers, blacksmiths, and skilled horsemen being ordered to report to the Army Service Corps Depot at Moor Barracks in Bradford. The suddenness of the call up meant that Hull Reservists many of whom had been in civilian life for several years were thrust straight into the frontline, including 30 Hull policemen. Numerous Hull men were in action at Mons on Sunday 23rd August; Gunner James Sharpe, a Reservist, was called back to the Royal Field Artillery whilst Pte. Arthur Hird, from Portland Avenue, Withernsea Street in Hull was serving with the Royal Army Medical Corps. Frederick Mileham has the distinction of being the first of around 7,000 Hull men killed during the war. Serving with the 18th Royal Hussars (Queen Mary's Own) he was injured at Mons, later dying from wounds on 24th August. Robert Wells, Coldstream Guards, James Kennedy, R.H.A and William Walker, K.O.Y.L.I were Hull men killed in the last week of August on the Retreat from Mons.

Leonard Frederick Instone, a Hull schoolboy swimming champion had just turned 17 when war was declared Andrew Ernest Elton, Jack Whitely and many others were just 19 and 20. There were many other older Hull men who were Reservists in their 30s, all serving together in the two Guards brigades in the critical early months of the war. Many of the men who were all wearing soft caps and fighting in the primitive and hastily dug trenches of 1914 would not survive the war. Those that did would see war change beyond all recognition. Gas would be used for the first time in the spring of 1915, whilst the tank would not make its debut until 1916. But it would be artillery shells that would be the biggest killer of the war.

Resting in the town square, men of the 4th Battalion Royal Fusiliers hours before the Battle of Mons

Steel helmets similar to those worn by English bowmen at Agincourt in 1415 did not become standard issue for all soldiers until 1916, when British industry was able to produce the first one million. The British Expeditionary Force who fought at Mons, Le Cateau, the Marne, the Aisne and the First Battle of Ypres had allegedly been mocked and underestimated by the Kaiser, due mainly to the tiny numbers of men they were bringing to the battlefield. The British soldiers who fought in the shallow, squalid trenches of 1914 would later become affectionately known as "The Old Contemptibles". The war could have so easily been over by September 1914 but it was the disciplined men of the BEF who would support the much larger French Army in checking the German advance at the Marne in September and ensured that a European conflict would develop into a World War, although the BEF would be decimated by December 1914. This left the Territorial Force numbering around 268,700 officers and men who had been trained primarily for a home defence role but found themselves left to reinforce the BEF in 1915, whilst Kitcheners New Armies were undergoing their first months of training.

Chapter One

The Checks and Balances Break Down Across Europe

By 1910, Europe comprised of two armed camps; the Franco-Russian Alliance and the Triple Alliance of Germany, Austro-Hungarian Empire and Italy, also known as the Central Powers. The Entente Cordiale Agreement in 1904 was more about Britain and France resolving their overseas rivalry in Egypt and Morocco but it had the effect of drawing two ancient enemies together, culminating in the Triple Entente of Russia, France and Britain in 1907. The huge standing armies of Germany, and France were almost entirely comprised of conscripts, the French Army numbering over 2 million men in 1914. The German conscript army amounted to almost 9 million men whilst the strength of the huge peasant armies of Russia, numbering millions, could only be guessed at. The cause of the First World War is far more complex than that of the Second World War and has been looked upon by some as an unnecessary conflict that Britain could have avoided. The Kaiser's war like rhetoric was often more theatrical than meant with conviction. His increasingly erratic behaviour in the summer of 1914 has helped to create a degree of uncertainty about who was actually to blame for the outbreak of the First World War and is still hotly debated a century later. The assassination in June of the Austrian Archduke Franz Ferdinand and his wife at Sarajevo in Bosnia, by a romantic Bosnian Serb and its immediate ramifications are not in doubt. Austria's desire to strike back hard at Serbia is not in doubt either but it is the lack of evidence and the unsubstantiated backing given to Austria by Germany, ensuring that Serbia was given an ultimatum they could not possibly accept that creates so much debate amongst historians. Known as "the blank cheque," this refers to the military backing allegedly given to Austria by Germany should Russia intervene on the side of fellow Slavs. Many argue that without this backing, Austria would not have felt able to take action against Serbia. It was Germany pushing Austria to attack Serbia that began the chain of events that lead to the start of the First World War. With France and Russia joined by a treaty this ensured that in the event of a war with Germany they would fight together. Sir Edward Grey, British Foreign Secretary, attempted to pacify Germany, as Prime Minister Neville Chamberlain would famously do at Munich some 25 years later. Grey envisaged that if war came, it could be limited to the Dual Alliance of France and Russia on one side with The Triple Alliance of Germany, Austria-Hungary, and Italy opposing them. After Austria-Hungary mobilised against Serbia and with Russian mobilisation taking many weeks, Grey still believed a European war could be avoided by military posturing and the mere threat of war.

Debate still rages about Britain's role and that if not honour bound by a treaty with Belgium, "The Treaty of London 1839," which guaranteed the country's independence, then it may have been possible to stay out of what was on paper an evenly balanced conflict. The lack of concern at Government level and in the British press towards a possible conflict in Europe is borne out by the fact that in July 1914 more pressing issues for Asquith's Liberal Government were Home Rule for Ireland, industrial strikes and the increasingly violent suffragette campaign. Barely mentioned in the Times and Daily Mail was the dramatic chain of events taking place across Europe after the murder of Archduke Franz Ferdinand and his wife at Sarajevo. By the end of July, war was being considered as a realistic possibility, with Britain's armed forces being put on standby whilst members of the Territorial Force were being ordered back early from their summer camps. But Britain would enter the European War late on a Tuesday evening to honour Belgium neutrality in a treaty going back seventy five years, with the first British troops arriving in France just ten days later.

The Schlieffen Plan

Devised between 1892 and 1905 by Alfred Von Schlieffen, the German battle plan was both offensive and defensive and made a war on two fronts against France and Russia inevitable. This was highly dependent on German rail transporting troops to the front on a tight time schedule, whilst access through neutral Belgium was an integral part of this two pronged plan. This would mean a swift and decisive victory over France within just six weeks, giving the German Army time to transport millions of troops to face the slowly mobilising Russians in the east. Time was essential for Germany. Whilst Britain's neutrality was uncertain, it had long been believed that she would enter the war and her small army was not taken seriously by Moltke, who was more concerned about the limitless numbers of the Russian Army. He argued that Germany must strike first and defeat France before Russia was able to bring her huge peasant armies to the Eastern Front. This plan meant that mobilisation led directly to war with the rapid defeat of France essential in the early weeks of war. It was the unprovoked German invasion of Belgium soil that ensured Britain would join the European War after the other major powers had become committed. The proposed plan of action was dependent on several assumptions. The first being that France could be defeated within six weeks, this was the length of time it was expected to take the Russian Army to mobilise. It was believed Belgium would not resist the German invasion, and Britain would remain neutral, although this was uncertain. The reality was that the Belgian Army and the BEF quickly resisted the German attack, whilst Russia was able to mobilise much quicker than expected, and Paris did not fall to the German Army.

The outbreak of war was initially confined to the European Powers with Serbia and Belgium becoming caught up in a conflict amongst much greater forces. Countries not at war in August 1914 would later enter the conflict often for territorial gains or

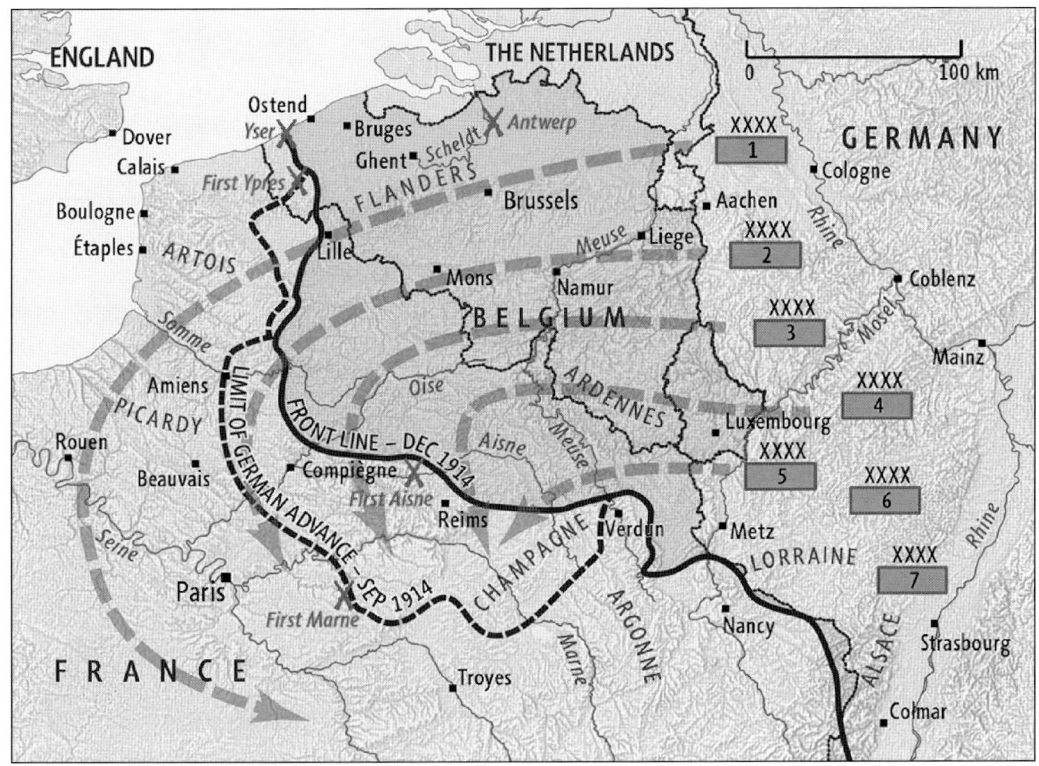

The German advance across France and Belgium in 1914

for the preservation of their empires and overseas colonies. Afraid that the Triple Entente of Russia, Britain and France would divide the ailing Ottoman Empire in the event of a military victory, Turkey particularly feared Russian domination. In 1914 Turkish Officers were being trained in Berlin under German General Liman Von Sanders who had been made a Marshal in the Turkish army and navy whilst military resources had been promised by Germany. Convinced that Germany would be victorious and that the Ottoman Empire would be preserved, Turkey helped Germany bombard Russia on the Black Sea aligning herself firmly with the Central Powers. Somewhat late to act Russia, France and Britain finally declared war on Turkey in November; had they acted earlier, they could have prevented the straits to the Black Sea from being significantly strengthened under German control.

Italy remained neutral at the outbreak of war but with the tempting prospect of acquiring the Tyrol and Istria she declared war on Austria- Hungary on 23rd May 1915. With rising tension and the prospect of losing her overseas colonies in Angola, Portugal offered to enter the war in August 1914. The offer was initially declined by Britain's Foreign Secretary, Sir Edward Grey, although Portugal, an old ally, would join the war after interning German ships in Lisbon. Germany declared war on Portugal in 1916 and Portuguese troops would eventually serve alongside men of the East Yorkshire Regiment on the Western Front during Ludendorff's Great spring offensive of 1918.

The Cardwell Reforms 1869-74

Between 1869 and 1874, Edward Cardwell, Secretary of State for War, undertook what were initially unpopular reforms for many British Army Regiments. One privileged but archaic tradition that came to an end was the purchase system for officer commissions. Men serving with the infantry had their active service reduced from twenty one years to seven with the colours, three on the reserve, and a further three with the colours and nine on the reserve for Foot Guards. The Cardwell reforms were forward thinking. Initially designed to modernise the British Army after the debacle of the Crimean War and Indian Mutiny, they were intended to attract a broader section of the population to the infantry whilst establishing a large reserve force. The reforms of the 1870s ensured most infantry regiments had two battalions, whilst the Foot Guards had three and some Rifle Brigades four. Two paired battalions for each regiment, 1st and 2nd, meant that one would be retained for home service, ensuring men could spend time with their families before serving overseas. By the outbreak of the Boer War on the 11th October 1899, many British soldiers had still received little training in marksmanship whilst more emphasis had been placed upon massed volley fire when faced with charging hordes of poorly armed native forces in Africa and the Sudan. However this was not an effective tactic when fighting a highly mobile European army equipped with modern arms. The debacle of the Boer War particularly in adopting modern infantry tactics ensured that the British Army later became a small but formidable force after a radical programme put in place by Secretary of State for War Lord Richard Haldane between 1906- 12. But it was the reforms that Cardwell had implemented during the 1870's, that had created a large reserve force, which meant many Hull men who had previously served in the British Army and navy were immediately called back to the colours in the first week of August 1914.

Edward Cardwell,
Secretary of State for War 1869-1874

The Use of Trench Warfare

The construction of trenches was a highly effective form of defence for smaller armies when facing superior forces. Trenches had been used in the Crimean War and in the latter part of the American Civil War when Confederate armies, facing much larger and better equipped Union forces, began to dig defensive fortifications at Vicksburg and Petersburg. More than 35 years later Boer forces in South Africa which never numbered more than 45,000 men used trenches to their advantage when facing the might of the British Empire. The Boers had constructed unseen narrow trenches around the Modder River and Magersfontein, using them to devastating affect against the massed ranks of the Scots Guards who advanced across open ground in what became known as "Black Week" for the British Army after three disastrous battles in December 1899. In what was becoming a rehearsal for the Great War, a Hull man, Sergeant William Traynor, serving with the West Yorkshire Regiment left the battalion trenches under heavy fire to bring in an injured man after a large Boer force launched a determined attack. For this action on 6th February 1901, Traynor was awarded the V.C.

In August 1914, a war of movement was envisaged and planned for by all armies, ensuring that troops were not supplied with spades and picks for entrenching. Having been trained primarily for an offensive war with heavy casualties expected, it was predicted to last just a few months. The first two months of the war were

Confederate trenches at Petersburg American Civil War

ones of movement with massed frontal assaults, although crude rifle pits and the first basic trenches of the war had begun to be constructed after Field Marshall Sir John French ordered the BEF to entrench with whatever tools they could commandeer from nearby farms on 14th September. These early trenches were poorly constructed, running in narrow lines and without sufficient depth snipers could pick men off who became exposed, whilst a shell blast could travel down the whole length of a trench. The War Diary of the 3rd Battalion Coldstream Guards, shows the vulnerability of men in the trenches, when on the 28th October 1914, four men were killed and over seventy wounded by active German snipers. The British Army handbook stipulated that a trench should have a depth of 7 feet and be a minimum of 3 feet 6 inches wide .The British trenches were usually inferior to those built by the Germans throughout the duration of the war. German policy for much of the war was to hold the land they occupied ensuring that they would invest more time digging deep trenches with bomb proof bunkers, a canteen and sometimes even cinema. British policy was generally one of offence meaning that the army was reluctant to invest time in the physical construction and use of materials in trenches which would later be abandoned.

Hull Boer War V.C winner, Sgt. William Traynor

British trenches along the Aisne in 1914

Chapter Two

Scarlet Tunics and Bearskins; Hull Coldstreamers in 1914

Hull men during the First World War are generally thought of as serving with the East Yorkshire Regiment. Their response was magnificent, raising four Pals Battalions in just 11 weeks during the opening months of the war. Whilst it is true that the majority of Hull men enlisted in the East Yorkshire Regiment, a less well known fact is that the Coldstream Guards had long been a favoured regiment for Hull men before the war, with several Reservists having served in the Boer War. The oldest regiment in the British Army, the elite Coldstream Guards, had been raised in Coldstream, Scotland in 1650 and became part of Cromwell's New Model Army. Being the senior regiment of the British Army they have been involved in almost all of this country's military engagements serving with particular distinction in the Crimean War at the Alama, Inkerman and Sevastopol, where they won four Victoria Crosses. The distinctive scarlet tunics of the British Army and in particular the Guards battalions had become relegated to ceremonial duty around Windsor and London after being replaced by a more practical khaki during the early 1880s. In contrast to most infantry regiments, the Coldstream Guards consisted of three regular battalions in 1914; it did not have any Territorial battalions, nor did it contribute to any of Kitchener's New Armies but it did form a Pioneer Battalion in 1915; the 4th. One popular myth associated with the Foot Guards is that men had to be a minimum of 6' feet tall but this was not true in the early years of the 20th century with Hull men Timothy Grant, Herbert Dearing and Joseph Bilton's enlistment medical records testifying to the fact that they stood 5 feet 10 inches, although many other men like Frederick Charles Ware and Sidney Warden were 6 feet in height. The practicalities of recruiting men that were all 6 feet tall in Edwardian Britain, when due to a poor diet and cramped housing the average man stood around 5 feet 7 inches would have not been realistic. This would have limited the army's intake, meaning they would have had to refuse the services of many good men.

Sgt. Timothy Grant,
Boer War Veteran & Reservist in 1914

Whilst the British Empire was at its zenith in 1900 the period between the end of the Boer War in 1902 and the beginning of the First World War was a relatively quiet time militarily for the British Army, who were engaged in a radical training and modernisation programme. No Victoria Crosses were awarded for a decade until the outbreak of the First World War but the British Army of 1914 was in far better shape than it had been in 1899. When mobilisation began on the 4th and 5th of August, numerous Hull men had left the army years earlier and had settled back into civilian life, many with several children. Of 368 Reservists who reported to 2nd Battalion Coldstream Guards Depot during that first week in August 1914, 165 men (44 per cent) were initially transferred to the 4th Reserve Battalion after being deemed unfit for military service. The Coldstream Guards consisted of three battalions in 1914, with a fourth Reserve Battalion raised at the outbreak of war which would go on to provide over 16,500 drafts for the three battalions. Hull Reservists were employed in a wide range of occupations in 1914; around 30 Hull policemen were called up for military service on 5th August. The British Army of 1914 was small in comparison to that of her continental neighbours. Reliant on the most powerful navy in the world which was starting to be rivaled by the Imperial German Navy in comparison the British Expeditionary Force that embarked for France was just over 100,000 strong.

Hull South African War Memorial erected by Public subscription in 1904

Feet that had not been accustomed to rigid army boots for several years would soon blister and swell as the British army marched hundreds of miles in the sweltering weeks of August and September 1914. Over 50 per cent of the BEF were made up of Reservists and more from amongst the Guards brigades. Based at Aldershot and Windsor, the three battalions of the Coldstream Guards landed at Le Havre on 14th August. To many people the immediate image conjured up by the Great War is of trench warfare fought across a muddy featureless landscape, lasting for years and killing millions. Much of this perception is correct, but the first two months of the war in August and September were ones of continuous movement, from Mons in Belgium to the Marne in north-east France. The huge clash at the Marne and the enormous French and German losses resulted in the pursuers being chased to the River Aisne, where the German Army scraped out formidable defences on the Chemin des Dames, resulting in a deadly stalemate that would last for years.

An infantry brigade in 1914 consisted of four infantry battalions, although this was reduced to three in 1918 due to heavy losses and under strength battalions. The 1st Guards Brigade, (part of the 1st Division in 1914), came under the command of GOC Sir Douglas Haig then a Lieutenant-General it comprised of 1st Coldstream Guards, 1st Scots Guards, 1st Black Watch, and the Queens Own Cameron Highlanders, numbering over 4,400 men. The 2nd and 3rd Battalions Coldstream Guards were part of the 4th Infantry Brigade 2nd Division and it was these brigades that would be involved in action around Mons, at the Marne, along the River Aisne and the First Battle of Ypres.

The Battle of Mons Sunday 23rd August 1914

At the time of writing in June 2015, we are just weeks away from the 101st anniversary of the Battle of Mons, that day will also be a Sunday as it was in 1914. The Battle of Mons is one military engagement from 1914 that is still remembered today. Eager to get to grips with the enemy, the action at Mons was a battle which suited the men of the BEF, who excelled themselves from their defensive positions against superior forces.

Many Hull men serving with the Guards battalions during August 1914 had been on the reserve and were immediately called back to colours at the outbreak of

The Town of Mons

war. One such man was Joseph Bilton who had joined the army in 1903 but had been back in civilian life for just several months when the call to arms came. Being an elite regiment in the British Army ensured that the Coldstream Guards embarked for the front just nine days after war was declared. Privates, John Albert Knowles, Harry Cook, George Harrison, Bernard Warcup and Leonard Frederick Instone were just a few of the Hull men serving with 1st Battalion Coldstream Guards whilst more than 90 other local men were with the three battalions. On 13th August, the 1st Battalion boarded the SS Dunvegan Castle at Southampton, disembarking at Le Havre the following day. The diary entries for the month of August tell of continuous daily marches in hot weather until 24th August, when the 1st Coldstream Guards were deployed to cover the retirement of the 3rd Brigade. The 2nd Battalion started marching at 3am on Sunday 23rd; two hours later they had crossed the Belgian frontier at Malplaquet, the site of one of the Duke of Marlborough's bloodiest victories 205 years earlier. By late morning, they had reached the village of Hyon on the outskirts of Mons, after which time they were then ordered into the firing line and to dig shallow rifle pits. In the early hours of Monday 24th the battalion which contained numerous Hull men was ordered to withdraw and form up with the 3rd Battalion Coldstream Guards to cover the retreat from Mons, before retiring and marching until 8.00pm with no casualties sustained. The Battle of Mons was the first major engagement of the war and has taken on an almost mythical status. In the run of engagements, its losses were small compared to future actions, around 1,600 suffered by the BEF whilst German casualties vary from 5,000 to a more conservative figure of 3000. Outnumbered almost three to one, the BEF fought well with their disciplined 15 aimed rounds a minute, known as "the mad minute", causing heavy casualties amongst the masses of the closely formed ranks of field grey clad German infantry. Both sides were able to take something positive from the first major engagement of the European War, with rapid British rifle fire checking the German advance. Heavily outnumbered, it meant I and II Army Corps were forced to retire from their defensive positions which then precipitated a desperate 160 mile fighting retreat during the following 12 days. The action at Mons and the subsequent retreat did have one positive effect, with more men arriving at local recruiting offices during September. But shortly after the retreat from Mons the first major action of the war involving the British Army a remarkable story sprung up, which would endure for decades. The legend of "The Angels of Mons" took hold after Welsh author, Arthur Machen, of the London Evening News, wrote a short article titled "The Bowmen" in September 1914. British soldiers falling back from Mons were alleged to have been aided in their retreat by phantom bowmen from Henry Vs army, who had won a famous victory against the French at Agincourt 499 years earlier. It is quite possible that many British soldiers retreating from Mons may have seen unexplained images. Dehydrated and deprived of sleep whilst marching day after day in hot weather some may have been hallucinating. Whilst no men reported it at the time, 50 years after the retreat from Mons there were a few veterans who claimed to have seen shadowy figures following their withdrawal, such was the power and longevity of the myth. Despite Arthur Machen later confessing that the article was a hoax, it had quickly become embedded in the British imagination. The public desperately wanted to believe in the story of the 500 year old bowmen of Agincourt coming to the aid of modern British soldiers at a time of crisis, whilst even the clergy requested copies for some of their parishes.

The sweltering summer sun of 1914 had the affect of physically draining the men of the BEF, who, after falling back from Mons, were often marching between 20 and 30 miles a day usually starting out in the early hours of the morning. With water strictly rationed, they were often not permitted a drink until mid afternoon. Through sheer exhaustion, many British soldiers literally slept as they marched, whilst some even began to hallucinate through fatigue and dehydration. The BEF were highly trained, capable of firing 15 aimed rounds per minute, but many were older men and having been away from the army for several years they suffered badly particularly in the retreat from Mons. Some soldiers fell out by the roadside whilst others begged their officers to let them stand and fight, such was the physical exhaustion and the pain of bleeding swollen feet often wrapped in their own puttees to lessen the pain.

The Battle of Landrecies 25-26 August 1914

After falling back from Mons, I Corps commanded by Sir Douglas Haig, retreated towards the town of Landrecies where Haig intended to establish his

headquarters. With the two corps of the BEF separated by the Forest of Mormal, II Corps headed to Le Cateau where General Sir Horace Smith-Dorrien, going against orders, chose to stand and fight in an attempt to check the pursuing German First Army and open up a gap on their pursuers. Although some 7,800 British casualties were sustained and 38 guns and dozens of horses were lost, the decision to make a stand at Le Cateau gave II Corps a buffer, allowing many to escape the desperate pursuit. The action at Le Cateau was the last time that British artillery fought in sight of the enemy, with the guns lined up wheel to wheel behind the infantry, as they had done at Waterloo a century earlier.

Belonging to I Corps were the 1st and 2nd Divisions, which contained the three battalions of the Coldstream Guards. Robert Wells had enlisted in the Coldstream Guards in 1903. He was Hull's first Coldstreamer killed in the Great War on the 25th August and is buried at Landrecies Communal Cemetery. During what was a very hot August day, over 90 exhausted men from the battalion fell out during the retreat from Mons. After reaching Landrecies, the Guards brigade were warned of the German advance by fleeing civilians. The Battalion War Diary states that when the attack began the leading Germans were reported as singing French songs and wearing French uniforms, whilst the men to the rear were dressed in German field grey uniforms. The town was attacked at 19.00 hours and the battalion pushed back with Pte. Thomas Robson, who was attending to the battalion's machine gun, being bayoneted. Crucially, the battalion lost one of its two machine guns at this point, forcing them to retreat through the town.

It was during the fighting at Landrecies, that the Coldstream Guards won their first Victoria Cross since William Stanlake and George Strong had been awarded the newly issued medal during the Crimean War 1854-56. George Harry Wyatt was a former Barnsley policeman serving with the Guards. He was awarded the V.C for twice braving German rifle fire to extinguish the flames of a burning haystack next to a barn, which was illuminating the Guards positions, leaving them vulnerable to rifle and machine gun fire during the hours of darkness.

Pte. George Harry Wyatt, awarded the V.C for action at Landrecies

Pte. 6107 Albert Teasdale, 3rd Battalion Coldstream Guards

Despite being driven back several times by controlled British rifle fire, the determined German assaults continued throughout the night, resulting in hand to hand fighting which only ceased during the early hours of the 26th. By dawn when they withdrew, 3rd Battalion Coldstream Guards had suffered casualties of 14 men killed and 105 wounded. One of them was Hull man Robert Wells his death was officially recorded as 25th August, meaning that he may have been killed early in the attack on Tuesday evening. An interesting fact noted in the Battalion War Diary is of the first use of German hand grenades, which were described as having the same effect as high explosive shells. Also involved in the desperate fight at Landrecies were Hull men Mark Lockwood and Albert Teasdale, who would both be fatally injured in action at the Marne just ten days later.

The exhausting Retreat from Mons lasted 11 days and demoralised the men of the BEF before General Joffre ordered the French Army to halt at the Marne on 3rd September. The Battle of the Marne stopped the German advance into France less than 30 miles from Paris, costing the French and German armies over 500,000 casualties whilst the BEF suffered around 12,000 casualties, including over 1,500 dead.

Fatally wounded at the Marne

After the death of Robert Wells at Landrecies, Albert Teasdale and Mark Lockwood were two more Hull men from 3rd Battalion Coldstream Guards to die early in the war after being wounded at the Marne, before the development of trench warfare had set in. The Hull Daily Mail incorrectly reported Albert Teasdale as the first Hull casualty of the war. Albert Teasdale had left the army in 1909 and by 1914 he was a married man and the father of two children, Albert Anthony aged two and Theresa

UDC War Memorial, Hallgate, Cottingham, East Yorkshire

Marguerita. A former resident of Finkle Street in Cottingham, he later moved to Hull and was living at 68 Raglan Street whilst working as a bricklayer when war was declared. As a Reservist, 30 year old Albert Teasdale was one of over 65,000 men called back to the armed services from across Britain on 5th August 1914. He was serving with the 3rd Battalion Coldstream Guards when he was wounded during the first week of September. Albert Teasdale died from gun-shot wounds to the abdomen on the 9th September and was buried in the churchyard at Boitron Seint-et Marne. He was one of one of two Hull Coldstreamers to die from wounds that day with Mark Lockwood, a former labourer from Courtney Street,-Holderness Road also losing his life on the 9th.

The Teasdale family moved several times around East Yorkshire during the early years of the 20th century, living at Hornsea, Hull and Cottingham. Sadly the family would lose a second member, Albert's younger brother Samuel. He was also serving with the Coldstream Guards when he was killed at the Battle of Pilkem Ridge, part of the Passchendaele offensive, in August 1917. Both Teasdale brothers are commemorated on the War Memorial at St Mary's Churchyard, Cottingham and on the village War Memorial located on Hallgate.

The Battle of the Aisne 13 -28 September 1914

Troops sent from Paris in French taxi-cabs, were some of those responsible for opening up a gap between Kluck's First and Second Armies, during the Battle of the Marne. Between 9 and 13th September, the exhausted German Army began falling back to the River Aisne. It was along the Aisne were they took advantage of the high ground on what is a steep and thickly wooded terrain very different to the flat and desolate battlefields which have become the surreal image of the Great War. In September 1914, due to lack of time and resources, four German armies dug shallow trenches commanding the heights of the Chemin des Dames. This was no casual position that the Germans had chosen, as they had surveyed the terrain before the war and were only too aware of the natural advantages that the Aisne heights held for defence. These trenches would be significantly strengthened by 1915 but it was around the River Aisne and its rugged valleys, that after less than a month, the British and French armies realised they would not be able to make a decisive breakthrough to the open country beyond. Trench warfare began at the Aisne but the battle is largely forgotten about today.

The Aisne battlefield stretched along a 100-mile front, although the BEF were only engaged on a sector of around 15 miles, whilst the river flowed along a two mile wide valley. Field Marshall Sir John French was initially unaware that German troops were digging in along the heights and ordered the 1st and 2nd Divisions to cross the river on the 13th September. With over 100 Hull men belonging to the Guards Brigades, six Hull Coldstreamers were amongst those killed in September whilst many more were wounded serving with the three battalions of the Coldstream Guards. After first crossing the Aisne on the 13th at Bourg-et-Comin, the following day 1st Battalion Coldstream Guards formed an advance guard and were directed north over the high ground between Vendresse and

The wooded terrain along the Aisne concealed German artillery and machine guns

Paissy. Later in the day, the battalion managed to take the village of Cerny-en-Loannois but with stubborn German resistance, a retirement took place as night fall approached. A final position north-east of Vendresse was secured before they were relieved during the night and went into reserve on the 15th. Casualties for 1st Battalion on 14th September were 364, with over 75 men killed or dying from wounds received that day.

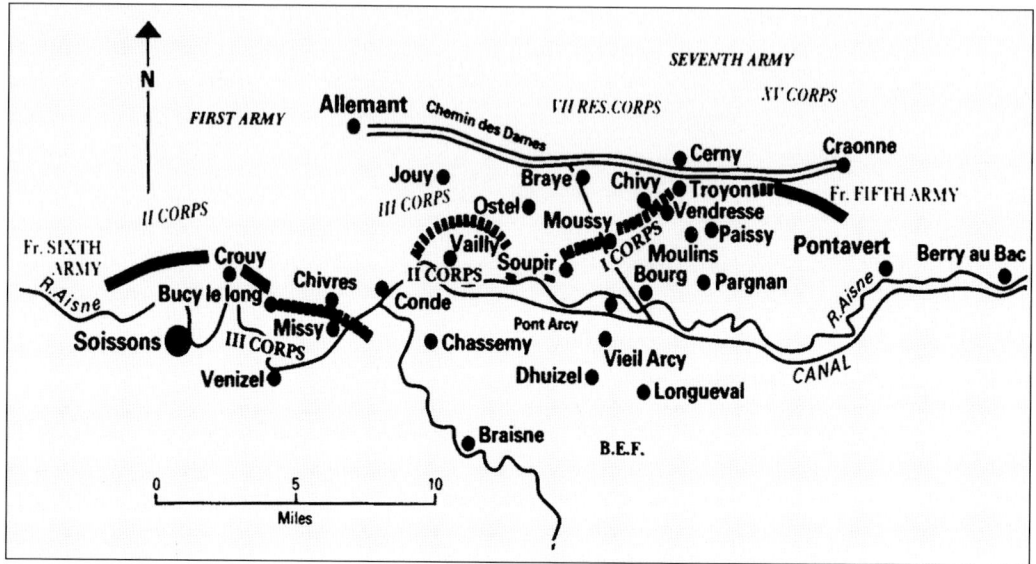

The Aisne Battlefield

Nineteen-year old Andrew Ernest Elton, from 1 Normans Terrace, Campbell Street, Hull was killed on the 14th, whilst Pte. Frederick Livingston Thorrold, another Hull Coldstreamer, was shot twice through the left arm. During the following days the battalion's casualties carried on rising with Pte. Harry Cook, from Newstead Street, in Hull, being one of those injured.

The 1st Coldstream Guards were reinforced on 20th September with the arrival of Lieutenant Viscount Acheson and 218 other ranks. Harry Cook's account and the hard time that the Coldstream Guards were having, was told to The Hull Daily Mail and featured in October 1914.

> *"Private Harry Cook from Newstead Street has lost a finger with another one badly injured after being wounded on 19th September he was moved to a field hospital. Cook estimated his battalion had suffered 600 casualties by the time of his evacuation. He spent three days travelling by train before arriving at St Nazaire from where he was shipped to England with another 1,200 wounded men onboard. Travelling with Cook were two injured Hull Policemen John Blyth and Harold Frederick Lyons who were both serving with the Coldstream Guards. John Blyth a well known Hull P.C stated he was not badly wounded and hoped to return to the front within a week or two, but he was glad of the rest after the grueling 160-mile retreat from Mons."*

Chapter 2 — Hull Men at the Front in 1914-15

Pte. Harold Frederick Lyons, Hull P.C wounded at the Aisne

All three battalions of the Coldstream Guards had gone into action along the River Aisne on 14th September. For many men this was their third battle of the war in as many weeks, leaving several Hull men dead and many others with wounds to the limbs which required their immediate evacuation to England, whilst it cost the BEF 10 per cent of their total strength during the month of September. Joseph Bilton, Andrew Elton, Albert Haldenby, Randall Kirk, Mark Lockwood, and Albert Teasdale were all Hull Coldstreamers killed in September. The heavy and superior German artillery including howitzers, outranged and out-numbered the British guns and with the advantage of the high ground on the Chemin des Dames, the BEF suffered over 13,000 casualties in just two weeks. The first heavy casualties came as a shock to the British public. In just over two weeks the army had suffered three quarters of the number of casualties that it sustained in over two and half years during the Boer War. The result of the Battle of the Aisne left the Germans still in possession of the high ground on the Chemin des Dames, whilst the BEF had secured a tenuous line along the Aisne which was vulnerable to heavy shelling. With the British and French unable to break through it brought the war of movement to an end, resulting in stalemate from Switzerland to the Belgian Coast.

Pte. Walter Kemp, wounded in the foot at Soupir

Hull Postman, Walter Blackburn, wounded at the Aisne

Pte. Joseph Bilton 3rd Battalion Coldstream Guards Killed at Soupir 16th September 1914

As well as the deaths of Robert Wells, Albert Teasdale, and Andrew Ernest Elton, Joseph Bilton was another Hull casualty serving with the 3rd Battalion Coldstream Guards. The Hull Daily Mail of October 1914 referred to him as "another Guard's victim". He was one of six Hull Coldstreamers killed in September 1914. Joseph Bilton was born in Hull in November 1887, and was educated at Fish Street School, Hessle Road. He enlisted in the Coldstream Guards in 1903. After eleven years service, he left the army in 1914. Like many former soldiers, some of whom later became Hull policemen, Joseph Bilton was employed in a position of authority after becoming the Labour Master at York Workhouse. He was living at the family home on 73, Arundel Street, near to Hull Prison, when he was called up at the outbreak of war just months after leaving the army.

On 14th September, the 3rd Battalion Coldstream Guards left their billets at 06.00 hours and crossed the River Aisne at Pont Arcy by way of a pontoon bridge. This had just been constructed under heavy artillery fire by the Royal Engineers to replace the original bridge one of many destroyed by German artillery and engineers in an attempt to prevent the British crossing. The 4th Brigade formed part of the left column under the command of Colonel Hall RFA, with 2nd Grenadier Guards forming the advance guard. The Battalion War Diary records that they were heavily engaged all day and during the night were subjected to heavy rain when the companies changed over in the trenches under the cover of darkness. During the 14th of September, 3rd Coldstream Guards suffered over 300 casualties whilst Joseph Bilton was killed in action two days later on 16th September at Cour de Soupir and is buried at Vailly British Cemetery. The action on 14th September cost I Corps over 3,500, men whilst 1st Battalion Coldstream Guards had suffered 364 casualties and 3rd Coldstream Guards around 350, not dissimilar casualty rates to those sustained by some regiments on 1st July 1916. On the 17th, the battalion suffered further casualties of 8 men killed and 39 wounded, with many of the injured being taken to the chateau at Soupir, which had been converted into a makeshift hospital and mortuary.

The Battle of the Aisne was dominated primarily by German artillery and bloody hand to- hand fighting, encompassing four distinct battles. One early casualty of war was the farming village of Troyon situated on the southern side of the Chemin des Dames ridge. In August 1914, the small village was made up of several farms and around 30 cottages, before it was shelled to complete destruction. The 1st Battalion Coldstream Guards held trenches north of Troyon, during the first two weeks of October 1914. The Guards forward observation post was named Fish Hook Trench due to its semi circle shape.

The ruins of Troyon 1914

Chapter 2   Hull Men at the Front in 1914-15

The path leading from Troyon towards Cerny en Loannois

With the inhabitants of Troyon displaced, or dead, the small village was never rebuilt and only scattered fragments remain today.

Due to the primitive state of the trenches in 1914, the dead were placed at the back of the parapet and during the hours of darkness all the companies would carry their dead for burial in a chosen area just behind the lines. Dire necessity ensured a dead man's boots and clothing were removed if in good condition. During the early days of the battle of the Aisne, due to the thickly wooded terrain and the lack of ambulances, many wounded men were often left were they fell. After being injured, those fortunate enough to be brought in from the battlefield were taken to regimental aid posts, which were often hastily prepared dugouts or abandoned farmhouses. Here their wounds were treated by orderlies of the RAMC. During the action at Soupir and around the farm on 17th September, over 40 men from 3rd Battalion Coldstream Guards were taken by ambulance to the Chateau at Soupir, which had been hastily turned into a make-shift hospital. The more seriously injured, were eventually put onboard filthy railway carriages, which transported them to one of the Channel ports. This could often take two to three days, before being shipped back to England which then took another 24 hours. Harry Cook from Hull, serving with the Coldstream Guards, was injured in September 1914. His four day journey back to hospital in England was typical of so many British soldiers. In an age before modern medicine and antibiotics, the dirty unhygienic conditions combined with a lengthy journey by rail and sea, led to many men dying from infected wounds. However great improvements in medical care were made as the war progressed. Many injuries were often not life threatening but debilitating leaving soldiers unfit for military service. Leg wounds were the most common injury, leaving some unable to march whilst for the more serious it often meant amputation. Hull Coldstreamer Sidney Warden, from Ruskin Street, Hull, who had served for several years, was one of numerous local men to suffer wounds to the legs or feet during the first weeks of the war when he was shot through the ball of the foot during action at Soupir. Thousands of soldiers in the first few weeks of war were out of action for weeks and months, although many would recover sufficiently to allow a return to the front before the end of 1914.

Some of the Hull Coldstreamers had long and distant family connections with the regiment often with brothers or previous generations having served. Bernard Warcup from Scarborough Street, Hessle Road, who was later taken prisoner, may have been influenced by his father's wartime experiences when he had served with the regiment during the Egyptian Campaign of 1885. There were several sets of Hull brothers serving with the Coldstream Guards in 1914, including the Gardiners, Haldenbys, Teasdales, the Smiths from Strawberry Street whilst the Harrison brothers were the sons of a well known Hessle Road shop proprietor. George was one of several Hull men wounded at the Aisne in September 1914.

George Harrison 1st Battalion

William Harrison 2nd Battalion

Gallantry awards

Private John Senior of the 2nd Battalion was one Hull man decorated for bravery in 1915. He was awarded the Distinguished Conduct Medal for an action on 28th October 1914. Senior was involved in going out into no-man's land and bringing in a wounded comrade, who had been left lying near to the German trenches for some considerable time. In November he was again involved in a similar incident. Lance-Corporal Leonard Robinson, who arrived in France in December 1914, was another local man who won the D.C.M. In July 1916, he was involved in rescuing officers and men from a deep mine full of poisonous fumes at great personal risk. The Coldstream Guards were awarded a total of 159 D.C.M's and 5 Bars during the war. The D.C.M was often awarded for the saving of life but Private Frederick William Dobson, 2nd Battalion Coldstream Guards, became the seventh V.C winner of the Battle of the Aisne and the second man from the Coldstream Guards to win the V.C since the Crimean War. The Regiment won two Victoria Crosses during August -September 1914, with George Wyatt becoming the first recipient and Private Dobson receiving the second award for saving a wounded man's life. General Sir Douglas Haig, who was not in favour of the highest award for gallantry being given for the saving of life, recommended the D.C.M. Haig was later overruled by the King and William Dobson was decorated at Buckingham Palace in February 1915.

Albert Haldenby was employed as a tram conductor by Hull Corporation in August 1914. The son of a Police Inspector from Beverley he had just completed seven years with the Coldstream Guards and had an older brother, Arthur, also serving in the same regiment as a lance- corporal. A married man, he had only recently left the army and had just finished furnishing the family home on Brooklyn Avenue, Perth Street when war was declared.

The 2nd Coldstream Guards were entrenched at the village of Chavonne, which had previously been held by the Germans before an earlier withdrawal. The last week of September was spent fortifying and digging new trenches. Private Albert Haldenby was killed during a week of relatively light casualties for the 2nd Battalion. There were reports about a man called Haldenby from a Hull soldier writing home to his family, stating that he may be nominated for the Victoria Cross but that was to be a different man Frederick William Dobson. On the morning of 28th September, Albert Haldenby was part of

Pte. Albert Haldenby,
2nd Battalion Coldstream Guards
Killed 28th September 1914

a three man patrol that ventured out towards the German trenches during thick fog but as the mist lifted, two men were hit by German fire. Private Frederick William Dobson immediately volunteered to go out and help the stricken men. He found Albert Haldenby already dead but was successful at bringing in another injured man. For this act Frederick William Dobson was awarded the V.C by the King in February 1915. From 25th October to 17th November, 2nd Coldstream Guards suffered losses of 2 officers killed, 5 wounded and 64 other ranks killed, with 151 wounded amounting to 25 per cent of a full strength Battalion. By December 1914 in some of the BEF battalions just one officer and less than 50 original men remained from the one thousand strong battalions that had landed on 14th August, whilst many had a fighting strength of no more than 300 men. On 17th November the 2nd battalion was relieved by French troops and went into General Reserve at Meteren, where in early December the companies received much needed reinforcements.

*John Albert Knowles,
1st Battalion Coldstream Guards
Died of wounds at Base Hospital,
Rouen 1914*

Unlike many of the Hull Reservists, John Albert Knowles, of 1st Battalion Coldstream Guards, was relatively new to the regiment, having enlisted in July 1913. From 28th September to 14th October the battalion held a front north of Troyon, with two companies whilst a further two companies were in reserve dugouts. The daily German bombardment was, for the most part directed to the rear of the Coldstream Guards towards the RFA positions although a few shells did fall on the two companies. During this time, there were casualties of 10 killed and 56 wounded. One of them was Hull man John Albert Knowles, who later died from his wounds. But it would be during the last week of October that the battalion would suffer its heaviest casualties.

Contrary to popular belief, many actions involved relatively few men, sometimes just a platoon or a company and not the thousands of men who took part in the great offensives of 1916 and 1917. On 4th October 1914, 2nd Lieutenant Merton Beckwith-Smith was ordered to lead one platoon in taking an advanced German trench which was just 100 yards from the Guards advance post. This may have been the first trench raid of the war. Trench raids were used later in the war to gather intelligence on the enemy positions and strong points whilst prisoners were often taken. With fixed bayonets, safety catches off and rifles carried at the slope, the attack began at 20.00 hours and involved 50 men, who were ordered to take and secure two German trenches. After the first trench was taken with the bayonet, a blast on the whistle was to be the signal for a party of 30 men to advance from the rear carrying shovels, with the O.C and sergeant belonging to the Royal Engineers directing the filling in of the position. In the first trench which had been abandoned the bodies of around 15 Germans were found, many of them having been killed just a few hours earlier by shell and sniper fire. After moving forward to take the second trench some 70 yards away, they were fired upon before 2nd Lieutenant Merton Beckwith-Smith gave the order to charge. Around 20 Germans were encountered in the second trench, outnumbered almost three to one they were quickly killed, many of them with the bayonet and rifle butt. The first man into the trench was Beckwith- Smith. He was brought down and shot through the arm and was about to be killed when Lance Corporal R. Russell shot and bayoneted the two Germans, saving the officer's life. When German fire opened up from a third trench and reinforcements could be seen moving up, having completed their two objectives, the order was given to withdraw back to their trenches, whilst it was deemed impossible to fill in the first trench which should have denied it to the enemy. Those men separated from the platoon and later, returning to the trenches, had been instructed to call out "Coldstream" to avoid been shot. During this action Beckwith-Smith and seven other ranks were wounded, whilst two men were missing believed killed in the German trenches. Despite the attack being successfully carried out, it aims were not achieved. Many operations that were conducted all across the Western Front often resulted in very little gain, or territory that would be later retaken. Merton Beckwith- Smith, Lance Corporal R Russell and three other ranks were recommended for their bravery with 2nd Lieutenant Beckwith Smith later awarded the DSO.

During action at Langemarck and Gheluvelt from the 21-29 October, the battalion suffered 30 killed with 93 wounded and 73 missing. Throughout the month of October, the 1st Battalion Coldstream Guards suffered very heavy casualties amongst its officers and men. Major The Honourable L.D Hamilton was one of 4 officers killed, a further 3 had been wounded and 10 were missing, whilst 6 officer drafts and 142 other ranks had been received to reinforce the battalion. Some of the Hull men from the 1st Coldstream Guards who were killed during the month of October were Lance- Corporal Andrew Gorman, Privates John Booker, Wilton Curwen, Percy Solomy Redhead, Fred Rispin and John Albert Knowles. Private George Perkins was posted missing believed killed in action but was later found to have been taken prisoner. By the 30th October the battalion had gone into Brigade Reserve near the village of Gheluvelt and had a fighting strength of just one officer and 80 men. Due to their weakened strength, they became attached to 2nd Battalion Coldstream Guards. A week later, on the 6th November, a much needed draft of one officer and 94 other ranks arrived. On the 28th November, the 1st Battalion was inspected and spoken to by Field Marshall Sir John French and the following day, Captain the Honourable J.B Campbell and 214 Officers and other ranks joined the battalion. The remaining days of November and the first two weeks of December were spent receiving new drafts and undergoing training before being involved in action around the village of Givenchy on 21-22nd December. At 3pm on the 21st December the battalion attacked with the Camerons alongside them. The Battalion War Diary states that the Germans were driven out of the village as far as the church. Casualties resulted in ten killed, 128 wounded and 57 missing. One of the men killed on the 21st was a former Reckitts employee, Pte. George Spires, he is commemorated on the Dansom Lane Shrine.

The First Battle of Ypres 19 October 22nd November 1914

In October and November 1914, the outcome of the war hung on the Battle of Ypres. For those men that survived the month of September and the action along the Aisne they would see far greater losses, with around 58,000 British casualties sustained at the First Battle of Ypres. The Battle of Ypres was fought in five stages by British, French and Belgian troops against the numerically superior German forces at Yser, Langermarck, Gheluvelt, La Bassée, and Armentières. By the 1st November, 1st Battalion Coldstream Guards were left with a fighting strength of less than 100 men. Despite having suffered casualties of hundreds of men, those battalions that had a fighting strength of 300 during the Ypres crisis were regarded as being up to strength. The strategically important town of Ypres held, but the losses devastated the small professional British Army whilst the "Race to the Sea" stalled blocking the German Army access to the Channel Ports. Four Hull men were killed on the 29th October whilst another 11 Hull Coldstreamers

Pte. John Charles Nicholson,
3rd Battalion Coldstream Guards

Pte. Fred Rispin
1st Battalion Coldstream Guards

Two of 15 Hull Coldstreamers killed during the First Battle of Ypres

died during the month long battle, which stretched from Arras in Northern France to the Belgian coast. Only with the onset of winter did hostilities diminish in what was a complex series of battles involving four armies.

John Charles Nicholson wrote to his mother back in Hull asking her to send him some cigarettes and matches which were constantly in short supply. He told her that there were several Hull policemen serving in his battalion. One of them, P.C Charles Baker, had just lost a finger to an artillery blast. Some of the Hull policemen, Nicholson may have known were Privates Frederick Ware, John Blyth, and Harold Frederick Lyons, all Reservists called back to the colours on 5th August. Despite the chaos and disruption of the war, the postal service remained very efficient with a letter from home taking on average three days to reach the trenches, which was extremely important for morale. Often it was the simple everyday pleasures that were the most prized; cigarettes were like gold dust and constantly in demand, whilst winter mufflers, socks and food stuffs of various kinds were all regularly sent through the post by relatives back at home.

Hull School Boy Swimming Champion

Leonard Frederick Instone was another Hull man from a military family. He was born in Belgaum India in 1897. His father, Louis, was a drum major in the East Yorkshire Regiment who had served in South Africa during the Boer War and at the outbreak of war in 1914, he was serving as a sergeant major with the 2nd Hull Pals. In 1911, the family was living at 16 Torrington Street in Hull with Leonard Instone attending Newland Avenue High School. Trained by Mr Lowery an accomplished swimming trainer he excelled and in 1911, at the age of 14 he had won the Hull Junior Swimming Cup, and was presented with a silver medal. In

May 1913, still only 16, he attested for service with 1st Battalion Coldstream Guards. He had been in the army just over a year and was still only 17 when he sailed from Southampton with his battalion, arriving at Le Havre on 14th August. He was one of numerous Hull men to suffer leg wounds in the early weeks of the war and with several other Hull Coldstreamers, he was sent back to England in September to recover from his wounds. It was during this time of recuperation that he attended and took part in a swimming event at Beverley Road Baths in Hull, where he had the chance to meet up with former schoolmates.

By 22nd October, Instone had returned to active service just as the First Battle of Ypres had begun. He was posted to the 3rd Battalion 4th Guards Brigade. During the next seven months he spent time in and out of the trenches, where he found a German officers luger pistol which he briefly kept as a souvenir. But it was on 1st May 1915, at around 9.00pm on a warm spring evening that he was killed by what was recorded as a stray shot to the head, whilst digging trenches in the farmland of Givenchy, seven miles from the town of Arras.

Hull Police Fighters at the Front

At least 10 serving Hull Policemen in 1914 were former Coldstream Guardsmen and as Reservists, they were called up at the outbreak of war. Well known in their close knit communities they were familiar faces to many Hull men and, like local sportsmen, they became minor celebrities at the front.

Frederick Charles Ware was one of the Hull P.Cs serving with the Coldstream Guards. Born in Hull in 1878, he started his working life as a fish packer on Hessle Road before enlisting in the 3rd Battalion Coldstream Guards on the 20th October 1899, just a week after the outbreak of the Boer War. For men accustomed to

Private A Anderson, serving with the 3rd Battalion Coldstream Guards, wrote home to his mother telling her about two Hull Policemen he was serving with, although he only mentions one by name.

"He was running alongside with me towards the German trenches when he went down after being shot through the leg, whilst P.C Charles Baker who works the beat on Carr lane was also shot but not badly injured.

military discipline, an occupational transition when leaving the army or navy was then to join the Police Force. After being discharged from the army in 1902, he went onto the army Reserve when he joined the Hull Police Force. Being a Reservist, he was called up on Wednesday 5th August 1914, when he reported back to the Guards barracks at Windsor. Like many other Hull men Ware was wounded in fighting in the early weeks of the war along the River Aisne at Soupir on 15th September. After being shot through the left thigh, he was evacuated back to England with several other local men, including three other former Hull policemen. Frederick Charles Ware went on to make a full recovery and was promoted to lance corporal in August 1915.

Hull P.Cs Harold Frederick Lyons and John Blyth being honoured by Superintendent Sharpe, October 1914

P.C John Blyth was a familiar face in Hull before the war and could often be seen on point duty along Whitefriagate and Queen Victoria Square. Living at home with his parents, 33 year old John Blyth was a Reservist in the Coldstream Guards and was called back to his former regiment on 5th August. John Blyth, Harold Lyons, Frederick Ware and Charles Baker were all wounded just a month into the war along the River Aisne and evacuated back to England in September to recover from their wounds. A week before returning to the front, P.C Harold Frederick Lyons and John Blyth, standing second right, were honoured by a presentation made by Superintendent Sharpe of the Hull Police Force at the Central Police Station on Parliament Street, Hull in October 1914. Of the 30 Hull policemen mobilised in August, around one third were serving with the Coldstream Guards in 1914.

L/Cpl Hill, former Hull P.C

After being wounded and treated for flesh wounds at a French hospital, L/Cpl P Hill found time to write home to his mother at the end of November 1914. He told her that they had been recently inspected by the Commander-in Chief, Field Marshall Sir John French whilst going on to say that there were just 200 men left from the original 1,000 strong battalion. He was of one around ten Hull policemen serving amongst the three Guards battalions and on the 18th November, he met another Hull P.C serving with the Coldstream Guards, when the 1st Battalion became attached to the 2nd Battalion due to the heavy losses it had suffered.

Edmund Hilliard had attested for Military Service in 1901 and was a serving Hull policeman from St Mary's Parish when war broke out. Like Hill, he had been involved in four battles within as many months. With the two men were two other Hull P.Cs, Herbert Dearing, and John Burton, although Hilliard would soon be sent home due to bad circulation in his legs, which may have been "trench foot" although he returned to the front in January 1915

The Gardiner family from Scarborough Street,-Hessle Road in Hull had three sons serving in the army in 1914. James a Coldstream Guards Reservist, was a policeman but serving in Grimsby when war was declared. Wounded at the Aisne he was able to write home from a hospital ship in 1914. His brother, Albert was also serving with the Coldstream Guards whilst another brother had joined the RFA.

By December 1914, the BEF had suffered over 90,000 casualties whilst almost one in three of the Hull Coldstreamers that I have recorded had been killed and one in two wounded by the end of 1914. Of around 225 Hull men killed in 1914 at least 29, more than 10 per cent, came from just one regiment, the Coldstream Guards. The deadliest month was October, with 11 local men being killed, 4 of them on the 29th. At least 15 Hull men were killed serving with the Coldstream Guards during the First Battle of Ypres, 19 October-22 November.

Robert Wells was Hull's first Coldstreamer to die in the war on the 25th August, whilst several Hull men were killed in late December. Despite an unofficial Christmas Day truce taking place on some sectors of the Western Front, Pte. Timothy Oliver, a former Hull Policeman who had been living in Walkington before the war was killed on the morning of Friday 25th and the following day Albert Raper, a Hull railway worker, lost his life. Sergeant Frederick Marshall of Portland Street was posted missing believed killed in action in January 1915. His death was confirmed on 25th.

The former Hull Police Station, Parliament Street, Hull

Casualty figures vary considerably and can be notoriously unreliable and sometimes misleading, with some men going unrecorded and others later dying of wounds, making exact figures often imprecise. B.S Barnes clearly makes this point in his book This Righteous War, explaining that Hull's heavy losses at Oppy Wood in May 1917 were initially estimated as hundreds of local men recorded as being killed but many were not Hull men. Whilst Hull's losses were very heavy, (on 3rd May over 100), many of the men from the East Yorkshire Regiment were not local men but drafts from other regiments after the heavy losses at Serre in November 1916. The casualties of 1914 are, for the most part inescapable and uncompromising with most battalions becoming skeletons of their August numbers and some being reduced to less than 100 original men and two officers. Of the 4,500 men who made up 1st Guards Brigade in August 1914, by 20th November there remained the following numbers, 1st Scots Guards 1 officer and 69 men; 1st Black Watch 1 officer and 110 men; 1st Camerons 3 officers and 140 men; 1st Coldstream Guards no officers and 150 men.

Numbers of Hull men killed serving with the Coldstream Guards during 1914

August	September	October	November	December	Total
1	6	11	6	5	29

Pte. Albert Raper
Hull NER Railway Worker Killed 26th December 1914

Whilst the heaviest casualties for the BEF occurred in October and November during the First Battle of Ypres, there were still around 11,000 during December, as the onset of winter helped to reduce movement and loss. The winter weather of 1914-15 was the worst in living memory; torrential downpours reduced the trenches to water logged ditches, whilst a bitter frost and falling sleet brought further misery in November. Working for the NER as a signalman at Hull Botanic crossing before the war, Albert Raper was a familiar face to many along Spring Bank. After spending much of November in reserve at Meteren whilst receiving new drafts and undergoing training, the 2nd Battalion moved to Le Touret, where they held trenches alongside the Grenadier Guards. Two companies of the battalion held a section of the front line trenches whilst one was in reserve and one in billets. The 24-25 December were bitterly cold days, with some men occupied in digging communication trenches whilst German snipers were active causing several casualties. After surviving the momentous battles of 1914 which decimated the BEF Albert Raper was killed on the 26th December and could be Hull's last Coldstream Guards casualty of 1914. He was one of 18 men killed and 42 wounded from the battalion during the last week of December.

The Guards Regiments were all based at Windsor and Chelsea in August 1914 and were different to many regiments because they were all immediately available to deploy for France, ensuring that they would all serve together in the first few months of the war. Required for ceremonial duties, the Foot Guards did not serve east of Suez. Most other infantry regiments that consisted of just two regular battalions had one overseas on garrison duty somewhere across the Empire, ensuring that the East Yorkshire Regiment and the Kings Own Yorkshire Light Infantry had just one battalion available that would see action during the first critical months of the war, limiting their casualties. In contrast, the three battalions of the Coldstream Guards were involved in almost all of the major battles throughout the duration of 1914 and it is hardly surprising that just a month into the war, the *Hull Daily Mail* was referring to the death of Joseph Bilton as "another Guards victim".

Taken Prisoner

Almost 50 per cent of those who served could expect to be killed or wounded but relatively few men, just less than 3 per cent of over five million men who served during the war were taken prisoner. Of those that were captured the vast majority were taken prisoner in the last two years of the war with 50 per cent taken in the last eight months, many during Ludendorff's Spring Offensive of 1918. Captain Cecil Moorhouse Slack M.C 1/4th East Yorks, who had served at the front since April 1915, was one of thousands captured in the spring of 1918, whilst Hull men John William Hobson and John West were taken prisoner at the First Battle of Ypres in October 1914. They were amongst the first 20,000 men who fell into German hands during 1914, whilst some 170,000 men were captured on the Western Front during the course of the war.

L/Cpl. John West, Boer War Veteran Taken prisoner November 1914, First Battle of Ypres

John West was one of the oldest men serving with 1st Coldstream Guards. Incredibly he had been a Reservist during Britain's last conflict, the Second Boer War of 1899-1902 and after being called up he was badly wounded at Diamond Hill in June 1900. By 1914 he was no longer a Reservist but chose to rejoin his former regiment on 2nd September. He embarked for France on the 7th October and was taken prisoner just weeks later during the First Battle of Ypres. His son was also serving with the Coldstream Guards in 1914. Both John Hobson and John West survived four long years as prisoners of war although with heavy casualties amongst the Guards brigades, particularly in 1914, their early capture may have inadvertently saved their lives.

The long established tradition of Hull men joining the Coldstream Guards meant that many of the city's first casualties came from the regiment. Involved in almost every major action in France and Flanders in 1914, they suffered some of the heaviest losses of any regiment in the British Army and were constantly in need of reinforcements during the first months of the war. Hull men continued to enlist in the Coldstream Guards throughout 1914 and 1915.This ensured that local men were supplementing the heavy losses and would be at the front in significant numbers as the war entered its second year. Unlike the men prior to August 1914, the new recruits were joining out of patriotic duty and not for a military career but for the duration of the war only.

New Hull recruits to the Coldstream Guards in 1915

Battle Honours for the Coldstream Guards in 1914

Mons 23rd August

Retreat from Mons 24th August

The Marne 5-12th September

The Aisne 13-28th September

The First Battle of Ypres 19 October 22nd November

Winter Operations

Chapter Three

Deadlock At The Aisne;
The First East Yorks Enter the War

The Cardwell reforms of the 1870's ensured that two paired local battalions would rotate home and Foreign Service duties between them, allowing men a period of home service with their families before being posted to India or Africa for several years. In August 1914 the 1st Battalion East Yorkshire Regiment was stationed at York, whilst 2nd Battalion was in Kamptee India and the 3rd Special Reserve Battalion was billeted at Victoria Barracks, Beverley. From the time of the Napoleonic Wars, local Volunteer Regiments and Militia Units had been raised for a home defence role. The two Hull Territorial Battalions, the 4th and 5th, were stationed in West Hull in 1914. After the declaration of war, the 1st East Yorkshire Regiment, commanded by Richard Erle Benson, left York for Scotland with a contingent of 27 officers and 957 other ranks. Although not a local man, Richard Erle Benson was well known and respected in Hull. Born in Middlesex in October 1862, he was the son of a distinguished Crimean War general. Educated at Eton, Benson began his military career in 1884 and was promoted on average every seven years, becoming the Battalion Commander of 1st East Yorks on 5th August 1911.

At the outbreak of the war, the 1st Battalion East Yorkshire Regiment was part of the 18th Brigade belonging to the 6th Division, commanded by Brigadier General Ingouville Williams, who would later be killed at Mametz in July 1916. He was one of 78 British Generals killed in the war. Initially retained for coastal defence during August, the 1st East Yorkshire Regiment, along with the 1st West Yorkshire Regiment, boarded the '*SS Cawdor Castle*' at Southampton on Tuesday 8th September and the following day, they were anchored off St Nazaire before disembarking on Thursday 10th. The Battalion War Diary states that several vehicles were damaged during the crossing, including machine gun limbers and a general service wagon. They were later repaired at St Nazaire, after which the battalion entrained for Coulommiers before marching towards the Aisne battlefield. In 1914 most battalions were issued with just two Vickers machine guns, which were capable of firing 450 rounds of .303 ammunition per minute. Many Regimental War Diaries in September 1914 tell of warm weather interrupted by torrential downpours. Serving alongside the two Guards brigades, the 18th Brigade, which included the 1st East Yorkshire Regiment and 1st West Yorkshire Regiment, were involved in action along the Aisne also known as the Aisne Heights. Similar to the Confederate trenches of the American Civil War exactly 50 years earlier, they were dug without proper entrenching tools in a matter of just days and weeks. The often

Lieutenant Colonel Richard Erle Benson, commanding 1st East Yorks 1914

crude and shallow German trenches along the Aisne with hidden machine guns became an effective obstacle at halting the British offensive during September 1914. Initially constructed in narrow lines, the German trenches along the Chemin des Dames would become a formidable defence by 1915.

The trench system in September 1914 consisted mostly of just the front line, whilst communication and support trenches began to be constructed as the lines expanded and developed. Communication trenches were required to move men and stores, whilst evacuating the wounded. The early primitive trenches of 1914 were little more than ditches which afforded men limited cover from rifle fire, especially when careless in their movements. Many were shot through the head by snipers when on lookout. A direct shell blast travelling down the full length of a trench afforded no protection at all, often killing or maiming several men in a row but as the war progressed, they were laid out in a zig-zag formation to lessen the affect of shell blasts, whilst traverses and firing bays strengthened the defender's position later in the war. But in 1914 the soldiers existed in the most basic and primitive trenches. Without adequate pumps they were often flooded for much of the time, with men often standing for hours sometimes knee deep in water, bringing on a condition which became known as "trench foot". This was just one of a number of terms which came into the English language during the First World War; others included "in no man's land" and "over the top".

German trenches 1914-15

1st Battalion East Yorks arrived at Bourg on the River Aisne on Saturday 19th September when they went into billets, later moving to relieve the Royal Sussex Regiment in their trenches.

Bourg-et Comin on the River Aisne

The battalion suffered its first casualty of the war to shell fire along a road being targeted by German artillery. This was just the first of many sustained during the coming days, which included five officers killed in September. Sunday 20th September was a day of heavy casualties for the East Yorkshire Regiment. With the West Yorkshire Regiment and the Durham Light Infantry on either side of them, the German advance was checked, but not before heavy casualties were sustained, culminating in over 73 killed, wounded and missing from the 1st East Yorks. One of the dead was a recently certificated marksman, Charles Edward Quaid from Beverley. The following two days saw heavy shelling after the battalion moved to relieve the Sherwood Foresters, with killed and wounded accounting for over 35 men.

Captain Eric Priestly Edwards, a 33 year old Scarborian and Lieutenant Basil Stewart Hutchinson from York were two officers from "B" Company killed on the 20th. Lieutenant Colonel Richard Erle Benson was seriously injured after leading

Pte. Herbert E. Hall, "A" Company
One of several Hull men killed on 20th September 1914

"A" and "B" companies in a counter attack which got within 50 yards of the German lines before he was shot down and the battalion was forced to retire back to their trenches. Hull men Joseph Welsh, Joseph Morton, Hilmer Poulson, Francis Knaggs, Herbert Hall, and Edgar Gardiner were killed on the 20-21st. Richard Erle Benson and Walter Herbert Young the battalion's two senior officers, had served together for over 20 years. In 1891 they were both gazetted to the rank of Lieutenant, when Benson became adjutant and Young vice adjutant. With his friend and comrade badly wounded, Major Young took over temporary command of the battalion. Richard Erle Benson later died from his wounds in the Base Hospital at St Nazaire on Sunday 27th September, when the battalion came under the command of the 1st Guards Brigade, who had then taken over the trenches of the 3rd Brigade. Shelling continued during the final days of September with the 30th claiming the lives of four men and ten artillery horses. As with many regiments fighting along the Aisne, the 1st East Yorks suffered heavy casualties, with injured Hull men Broughton and Hutchinson evacuated to the Seaman's Hospital in Greenwich. By the end of September Field Marshall Sir John French was in no doubt that the deadlock around the Aisne could not be broken and a withdrawal began in late September, with the intention that the Germans could be outflanked initiating what became known as "The Race to the Sea". After the action along the River Aisne the East Yorks began a series of movements which included marches by night, resting in billets and finally being transported by rail, which lasted around two weeks in total. The 1st Battalion East Yorkshire Regiment, part of the 18th Brigade became involved in the Battle of Armentières, which lasted from the 13th October-2nd November 1914. Then the monotony and stagnation of trench warfare began.

Pte Thomas Boddy enlisted in 1905. He served until 1913. After leaving the army, he went to work for Thomas Wilson Sons and Company as a chronometer maker. A Hull Reservist, Thomas Boddy was shot dead on the 13th October whilst giving covering fire for wounded men from his section. The 1st East Yorks contained hundreds of men with years of service in India and South Africa.

Pte. Thomas Boddy

Heavy losses throughout October included 72 casualties on the 18th, when the battalion encountered stiff German resistance after advancing to take Capinghem; Hull men killed on the 18th, were Charles Hodges, John Howard, John Bond, James Robinson, and Louis Farmery. Two days later, Reservist Harry Rands Parrott from Clifton Street in Hull was one of several local men killed from amongst 133 casualties, with 49 of them posted as missing after the Germans counter attacked. He had previously served in Burma and India with the 2nd East Yorks, before finding work at the Swan Flour Mill. On Tuesday 27th October, the battalion was subjected to a terrific bombardment of their trenches, killing 8 men and wounding 40, whilst the following day a counter attack was made inflicting over 200 casualties on the Germans and driving them from a captured trench. Over 350 men, more than one third of the battalion, became casualties during October, with around 25 Hull men killed in action and others later dying of wounds. The action of the 27-28th brought a message from brigade expressing their pleasure and satisfaction at the way in which the battalion had conducted operations during the previous two days, although another six Hull men were killed on the 28th. Losses for the 1st East Yorks were not dissimilar to many other battalions suffering casualties during October and November 1914. On 11th November, Lieutenant-Colonel William Herbert Armstrong arrived from India after leaving the 2nd Battalion East Yorkshire Regiment and took over command from Major Young. Often in warfare, soldiers fighting in remote rural areas name their location, or the battle they were involved in, after what they could see directly in front of them. In November the 1st East Yorks were dug in on a low lying boggy section of farmland along the Lys Valley which subsequently became known to the battalion as "Dead Cow Farm" for obvious reasons. At Gallipoli from 6-10 August 1915, the Australian attacks on the Turkish trenches across an almost barren treeless landscape became known as "the Battle of Lone Pine," which is also self explanatory. Only with the onset of winter did hostilities diminish as priorities changed to combat the rain and snow in November and December, although sniping continued unabated. On the 8th December, the War Dairy of 1st East Yorks describes the dire state of the trenches. The recently dug communication trenches were knee deep in water which was beginning to freeze whilst part of the parapet had collapsed with sandbags being used to support parts of the trench". With no outlet for water to drain away and primitive trench pumps, water quickly built up and sat in the bottom of the trench. With continual rainfall it turned the trenches into a sticky, sodden quagmire, making any movement slow as troops moved along the line.

Primitive German trenches in 1914

Sport across Hull in 1914 was at least as popular then as it today. Despite the heavy casualties and loss of life, Hull men at the front were still eager to learn of local football and rugby results. Private C Hart from Courtney Street was serving with 3rd Battalion Coldstream Guards and despite the very heavy casualties amongst the Guards battalions, he wrote home to his mother disappointed after finding out Rovers had lost to Wigan, Hull had lost at Bradford whilst only Hull City had won. Corporal M. Maichinock, who was serving with the 1st East Yorks, wrote to his brother on Buckingham Street, Holderness Road, stating that John Charlie Brain, a Rovers player, had been killed serving with the West Yorkshire Regiment on the 20th September whilst he had actually been wounded and was in hospital.

It was typical for several brothers or two generations of the same family to be serving with the East Yorkshire Regiment. Both father and son of the Barrass family from Spring Street in Hull, were serving with the 1st and 3rd Battalions of the EYR. The 8th December was a relatively quiet day with the only reported action being two active German snipers, which led to the death of Pte. Alfred Leonard Barrass from Hull, one of five local men from the battalion killed or dying from wounds in December. He was shot dead when undertaking trench fatigues, which included carrying water along the trenches whilst two days later another Hull man, James Barney was killed. On the 11th December, the battalion was relieved in the trenches by the North Staffordshire Regiment and undertook a precarious withdrawal along sticky, sodden trenches whilst having to be constantly vigilant of snipers as men slogged along the line. On 12th December the men went into General Reserve for two weeks and were billeted at Armentières, whilst on 22nd December half the battalion obtained much needed hot baths and were issued with clean clothing. Pte. Sam Langrick, a former joiner, was able to write home to his parents on Wellsted Street, Hessle Road in Hull, briefly describing their conditions but unable to give his present location. However like so many other soldiers he was desperate for a supply of cigarettes and news from home.

Pte. Alfred Leonard Barrass killed by a sniper

> *"Just a few lines to let you know I am in the best of health and up until now have managed to escape injury. As for my whereabouts I am about as wise as you, for where we are or where we are going we know nothing. We have been having a pretty rough time of it, lumpy beds when out of the line, and can only get a wash and shave occasionally, sometimes less than once a week so you can imagine how lousy we feel. At the moment we have been able to take a hot bath and clean clothing has been issued which has raised our spirits. I would be glad if you could send me some cigarettes, cigarette papers, some soap and a football paper or two".*

Officers

Whilst the purchase system for officer commissions had been abolished more than 40 years earlier, the Officer Training Corps in 1914 still relied almost entirely on young men from the landed gentry or the upper middle classes, who had all been educated at public school. Eton College lost 1,000 old boys, one in five that served as officers were from the school during the war. After the outbreak of war, many newly commissioned officers went straight to the front, where they joined their battalions with little prior training or a limited idea of what to expect. This is just one reason for their heavy losses. Expected to inspire and lead by example, many battalion officers of all ranks were usually at the front of an attack. They often displayed a total contempt for their own safety which led to heavy losses that were out of all proportion to their numbers. This is clearly displayed by the 4th East Yorks first action of the war on 24th April 1915, when the C.O, Lieutenant Colonel Shaw and two company commanders were among 15 men killed when leading from the front. As the war deepened the traditional source for replacement officers became exhausted, with educated men from the world of commerce and industry being recruited to supplement the losses. But the officers serving in 1914 were almost entirely drawn from the old world of military families, (such as Richard Erle Benson) and the landed gentry, which were often one and the same. A clear example of this is to be found in the 1914 War Diaries of the Coldstream Guards, with many titled officers joining the regiment. Many of these inexperienced but highly courageous officers leading their companies and platoons into battle for the first time, with very little training, simply did not have the time to learn and adapt to trench warfare before they were killed. By the spring of 1915, an attempt was made to give officers of Kitchener's New Armies a brief taste of trench life when they spent time in the front line for 24 hours. These tours were named "Cooks Tours".

On 1st October 1914, the First East Yorks was left with 17 Officers and 985 other ranks after they received their first reinforcements. This was 18 more than they had had after disembarking at St Nazaire but they were 10 officers down and October was a costly month for officer casualties, with Lieutenant Mark Robinson Pease from Hull being one of those killed on 20th October. Fighting on the 28th October cost the lives of a further four officers including one major, two captains and a lieutenant. In a full strength battalion at the beginning of the war, the ratio of officers to other ranks was around 40-1 but weeks into the war, casualties killed, wounded and missing could equate to one officer for every 20 men. Around 37,000 officers were killed during the War. The Prime Minister, Herbert Asquith lost a son. The author Rudyard Kipling's only son, John died at Loos whilst Queen Elizabeth the Queen Mother's brother, Fergus Bowes-Lyon was also killed at Loos in 1915. With casualties out of all proportion to their small numbers many battalions were desperately short of officers. By the end of September 1914, the 1st Guards

Brigade and 2nd Infantry Brigade had both lost three out of four of their battalion commanders whilst 561 officers became casualties during the Battle of the Aisne, amounting to one officer for every 22 other ranks killed, wounded or missing.

By December 1914, Major Walter Herbert Young was just one of six of the original officers still serving with the 1st East Yorks, from the twenty seven who had sailed from Southampton on the 8th September. Thirteen were dead just four months later and eight were wounded or missing. If the war had a positive outcome for those surviving officers wanting to make the army their career, then it ensured rapid promotion. Walter Herbert Young a very capable officer and Boer War veteran, had taken 18 years to reach the rank of major whilst Merton Beckwith-Smith, a 2nd lieutenant in the Coldstream Guards in 1914, had risen to the rank of major by 1917.

Chapter Four

Taking the King's Shilling
Hull Volunteers in 1914

The creation of the Hull Pals began in late August 1914 after Lord Nunburnholme the Lord Lieutenant of the East Riding was requested by the War Office to raise as many men as possible from Hull and across the region on a voluntary basis. Whilst the recruiting of Hull men into the Pals Battalions is well documented, many other local men were joining a wide range of different branches of the armed services. Men joined regiments for many reasons some to serve alongside family members or friends, (often the biggest reason), or others because of trade or a particular connection. A degree of patriotic rivalry began to develop across the city from the outbreak of war and was played out in the local press as clubs, workplaces and streets began to compete against each other. The Lincoln Street football team from Sculcoates had to be disbanded after eight of the team enlisted en masse in the RAMC in October 1914. The Brown, Farrah, Featherstone, Lynch, Parker, Tock and Whittle families were just some of those from Hull who had all provided five or more sons to His Majesties Armed Forces by 1915. A spokesman for the residents of Maple Street on Queens Road proudly stated to the *Hull Daily News* in April 1915 that they held the record for the number of Hull men enlisting, with 24 men having joined up by March 1915, 12 of them coming from just 4 houses along the street. It was estimated that over 19,000 Hull men had enlisted by the spring of 1915. Across the River Humber in the Lincolnshire town of Barton, it was estimated that around 300 local men were serving on land and sea by December 1914.

During the early months of the war the fate of little Belgium and the atrocities carried out by the Germans became part of an orchestrated national propaganda campaign. Locally the bombardment of Scarborough in December handed the recruiting authorities with a strong and just cause which was used

The legal quarter on Parliament Street, Hull, provided some of the city's first troops to the front in 1914. Around 30 Reservists who were serving as Hull police officers were called up in August 1914, whilst three men from Sandersons Solicitors joined up in the first few months of the war.

across East Yorkshire to drive men to the recruiting offices, with thousands of men flooding to enlist throughout December and January as recruiting figures in general began to diminish.

The poster of Kitchener with his pointing finger was displayed on thousands of hoardings and buildings across the nation from September 1914, although there were over 200 different designs issued and approved by the Government Recruiting Committee. Many showed various sections of the community with some displaying women encouraging their husbands and boyfriends to enlist. Others featured children, asking their fathers what they had done in the war, whilst old men were depicted expressing regret that they were too old to enlist.

Belgian Refugees

"Brave little Belgium" had resisted the German invasion for a vital six weeks, even turning on the sluice gates to flood parts of the land to deny it to the Germans. In reprisals, the medieval university town of Leuven was deliberately ransacked and vandalised by rampaging German troops, who set fire to the university library destroying over 250,000 medieval manuscripts, whilst over 300 civilians were rounded up and shot for allegedly firing upon German troops. Due to its close proximity, around 250,000 Belgian civilians fled to England, with many arriving in Hull in the early months of the war. Most of them were women and children who had lost everything. The Hull Committee responsible for relief was established on 7th September to provide aid, whilst clothes were donated, with food and lodging given freely by many from across Hull. Of the 500 volunteer helpers, 400 of them were women. By March 1915, the total amount collected for the Belgian Relief Fund from across the region was £7,743- 5s, with some of the donations coming from

Hornsea Parish Church and Mothers £3-7s,

Hull Association of Tug Owners £1-12s

Wesleyan Sunday school £8-10s

Thomas Wilson Sons & Co £15-2s

Similar to war refugees fleeing persecution today, they were granted asylum but more than 30 years before the creation of the Welfare State and with no government assistance available they relied entirely on voluntary aid throughout the duration of the war. Much of the assistance came from Peel House on 150 Spring Bank, from where blankets and clothing were collected and distributed. With a shortage of male labour in agriculture across the region, some Belgian men managed to secure work on local farms across the East Riding.

The logistical affects of the war impacted immediately on towns and cities across the country, whilst many faced huge problems of billeting the thousands of new recruits and providing food and essential resources. For some rural and coastal towns across the region, the influx of hundreds and thousands of recruits was a welcome source of local revenue at a time of great economic instability. At the outbreak of war, several of East Yorkshire's landed families became immediately involved in the recruitment and the training of new recruits and the establishment and funding of V.A.D hospitals. Lady Nunburnholme was very active from the outbreak of war. She was instrumental in establishing the headquarters of the Voluntary Aid Detachments for Hull and the East Riding at Peel House, 150, Spring Bank, whilst Mrs Strickland Constable and Lady Sykes became involved in the equipping and running of local V.A.D Hospitals. The work and organisation carried out at Peel House was paramount in establishing three V.A.D Hospitals in Hull, together with the distribution of clothing and food parcels sent to troops overseas and men in German prison camps. Volunteers were taught basic nursing skills, whilst several first aid stations were set up across the city. With the Yorkshire Coast being regarded as a possible location for an enemy invasion the 3rd Reserve Battalion Lancashire Fusiliers left Bury for Hull on 8th August, to perform a home defence role along the Yorkshire Coast.

Miss Brown and Miss Wood of the Hull Rest Station canteen in 1914

With thousands of new recruits and troops passing through Hull, the Rest Station Canteen was established along Paragon Street in September to provide food and refreshments. It was managed and run by Miss Brown and Miss Wood, two V.A.D volunteers.

The strict class division of the post Edwardian era ensured that the first Pals Battalion to be formed in Hull was the 'Commercials,' with recruitment commencing on 1st September at Wenlock Barracks on Anlaby Road. Less than a week later the battalion had reached its full strength and recruiting closed whilst the 2nd and 3rd Battalions were raised during September. Overwhelmingly middle class and educated, the 10th East Yorkshire Regiment drew men from the world of commerce, with office clerks, accountants and teachers joining the ranks. With so many men contained in the battalion being used to delegation, many were recognised as capable of holding the King's Commission and the rank of junior NCOs. In August 1914 there were 12,700 officers available for the regular army with around 9,000 for the Territorials. The rapid formation of the new Pals Battalions meant that there was a desperate need for experienced former NCOs and Commissioned Officers to lead and drill the new inexperienced battalions which were being assembled across Hull in the first three months of the war. The Northern Command were responsible for recruitment across the region and with the Lord Lieutenant they jointly approached Mr Douglas Boyd, a senior officer with Hull Corporation, to take over as Recruiting Officer at what would be the new venue for recruitment in central Hull. The Hull City

Wenlock Barracks, Anlaby Road, Recruitment and Training Centre in 1914

Hurry Up and Enlist!

TERMS OF SERVICE, Etc.

	Battery Q. M. Sgt.	Cl.	S.	Cpl.	L. Cpl.	Trooper or Pte.
Pay to Soldiers on Enlistment, per day	4/2	3/6	2/4	1/8	1/3	1/-
Allowance to wife per day (from War Office)			1/1 per day			
Do. (deducted from Soldier's pay) ...			at the Soldier's discretion.			
Do. per child, per day (from War Office)			2d. per day, per child.			

In addition to these a soldier serving abroad has 6d. a day deducted for his wife, and 1d. per day for each child, total not exceeding 9d. per day unless the soldier wishes. If the soldier wishes he can have the balance of his pay paid to his wife or dependants

PENSIONS to Widows and Orphans of Soldiers:—

Staff Sergts.	9/-	weekly for	Widow.
" "	2/-	" "	Each Child.
Sergts.	7.6	" "	Widow.
"	2/-	" "	Each Child.
Corporals	6/-	" "	Widow.
"	1/6	" "	Each Child.
Privates	5/-	" "	Widow.
"	1/6	" "	Each Child.

According to circumstances allowance is made by the Soldiers' and Sailors' Families Association.

NOTICE.

WANTED—Ex-Soldiers from 19 to 45 years of age.
        Others   ,,   19 to 35   ,,   ,,
Height: 5ft. 3 inches and upwards.
Chest measurement: 34 inches and upwards.

Go and enlist NOW.

THE CALL TO ARMS.

WHERE TO JOIN IN HULL AND DISTRICT

Appended are the recruiting offices, which are open all day, in Hull:—
PRYME-STREET;   WENLOCK BARRACKS;
CITY HALL;   HOLDERNESS-ROAD;
AND THE R.A.M.C. HEADQUARTERS, WALTON-STREET.

Hall was opened for recruiting purposes on 6th September 1914 and three days later the 2nd Hull battalion was raised. The central location of Hull City Hall and its spacious proportions were two important reasons why it was so successful in recruiting so many local men in the first few weeks and months of the war. Despite its central proximity accessible to so many men, tramcars with recruiting staff onboard travelled daily around parts of Hull, giving volunteers a free ride to the Hull City Hall so that they could enlist immediately. In the early weeks of the war new recruits were drilled in the main hall whilst its location meant it became a rallying point for hundreds of local men with many rousing speeches being given from the balcony. During the autumn and winter of 1914, route marches of 20 miles were regularly taking place through Hull and across East Yorkshire helping to build up morale whilst developing the fitness of the new recruits. Hull was becoming an armed camp, with many thousands of new recruits and servicemen passing through the city. The drilling of new recruits through the city soon became a common sight for the population, with parades taking place on Walton Street Fair Ground, Corporation Fields and Anlaby Road Cricket Ground.

The unofficial names given to the Hull Pals Battalions were the "Commercials", "Tradesmen", "Sportsmen" and "T Others". Hull's last Pals Battalion, the 4th Hull Pals, 13th E.Y.R, was raised in November 1914. The four Hull Pals Battalions

Taking the King's shilling, new recruits to the "Commercials" 1st Hull Pals

are often referred to by their service numbers or sometimes by their battalion number within the East Yorkshire Regiment, which can make it confusing. Being part of Kitchener's Service Battalions, raised after his initial appeal for 100,000 volunteers in 1914 they were often referred to as the first, second, third and fourth service battalions, whilst becoming officially known as the 10th, 11th, 12th and 13th Battalions of the East Yorkshire Regiment.

In what was rapidly becoming a gunner's war, the Hull Recruiting Officer, Douglas Boyd, appealed for men with specific skills to form local artillery units. Former artillery men who had not been recalled saddlers and men with equine skills, were appealed for to form local artillery units, which resulted in three Heavy Batteries being raised. Lieutenant Colonel Hall was successful in establishing the formation of the Royal Volunteer Garrison Artillery companies across the East Riding. Reserve battalions were essential in providing trained soldiers as drafts for the regiment overseas whilst releasing large numbers of regular troops back home for front line service.

The success of local men joining the East Yorkshire Regiment ensured that besides the two regular battalions the 3rd Reserve and the two Territorials 4th and 5th, a further seven battalions were added to the regiment by November 1914. Many local companies actively encouraged their employees to join up, often with the promise that they would be able to return to their former jobs immediately after the war was over.

Kingston upon Hull, the country's third largest port, had a population approaching 290,000 in 1914. At the outbreak of war, men left traditional industry and local firms from across the city including Reckitts, Needler's, Gough and Davy, the Hull Flour Mill and Thomas Wilson Sons & Co, whilst 50 members of the Wesleyan Chapel on Anlaby Road enlisted.

Besides the thousands of local men employed in the maritime industry the two railway companies, the North Eastern Railway and the Hull and Barnsley, were two of the biggest employers of Hull men in the late 19th and early 20th century. Pte. John Jenkins was one of thousands of Hull railway workers who would serve during the war, whilst around 400 Hull men would be killed from the North Eastern Railway and the Hull and Barnsley Railway. Employed by the NER as an engine shunter at Drypool, Jenkins was serving with "D" Company 1st East Yorks. In 1914 he wrote home to his wife after being taken prisoner, one of 49 men posted as missing on the 20th October. With so many men employed by the NER, they were able to raise their own battalion entirely for employees of the company the 17th Northumberland Fusiliers, with some 2,236 men from the company being killed during the war. Despite the numbers of railway workers volunteering, (some 17 per cent by 1915), it had been agreed with the War Office as early as September 1914 that those wishing to enlist must seek consent from their employers before enlisting.

Most regiments had a Special Reserve Battalion back in Britain to act as a feeder battalion to provide drafts for casualties sustained overseas. The 3rd Reserve

Hull NER Worker John Jenkins, Taken prisoner during the Battle of Armentières 20th October 1914

Battalion East Yorkshire Regiment was based at Victoria Barracks, Beverley in August 1914 but later moved to Hedon, where training was supervised by Lieutenant Colonel Stickland-Constable. The battalion was essential in providing trained men to replace those killed or wounded. Despite the shortage of officers at the front Kitchener realised from the outset of the war that it was essential for two or three officers from every battalion to be left back at the depot along with several NCOs to train the new raw recruits. Back in the market town of Hedon, two miles east of Hull, drafts were leaving to reinforce the battalion on the 7th October 1914, when one officer and 56 others ranks left for the front, with further reinforcements leaving in the last week of October and again in the first week of November.

Whilst a rigid class system existed in 1914, in which men were very aware of their place in society, this did not influence the numbers of men from all social classes joining different branches of the armed services. Reginald Anthony from Somerscales Street, Beverley Road was employed as a clerk at Sandersons Solicitors on Parliament Street at the outbreak of war, whilst several prominent Hull solicitors were also serving. He enlisted in 1914 in the 1/5th East Yorkshire Regiment, a Territorial battalion retained for home defence throughout the duration of the war. Anthony was serving with the 8th East Yorks when he died from wounds aged 22 on the 18th August 1916. He is commemorated on panel one of the Thiepval Memorial to the Missing of the Somme.

Another Sandersons employee was George William Willey of Durham Street, Holderness Road, Hull, who attested for service in the 2nd Hull Pals East Yorkshire Regiment on 12th December 1914. George Willey was reported as missing believed killed in action on 3rd May 1917 at Oppy Wood. He was one of over a hundred Hull men killed at Arras on that date, whilst over 56 lost their lives from the 11th Battalion and many others were wounded and missing. William Sharp Jackson was the third man to lose his life from a small Hull firm of solicitors. After the deaths of three of his employees, Harry Sanderson, a staunch Methodist who had founded Sandersons Solicitors on Parliament Street in 1911, continued to help support the men's families after the war.

Reginald Anthony, Sandersons Solicitors Clerk

Reginald Anthony
After enlisting in 1/5th East Yorkshire Regiment in 1914

Hull Seamen

If the war on the Western Front in 1914-15 left the British Army and its Victorian Generals struggling to adapt to a modern industrial war and break the trench stalemate, then the Royal Navy fared little better in combating the unseen menace of the German U Boat campaign. Britain was first and foremost a naval power. The Grand Fleet ruled the waves in 1914, although it had begun to be rivaled by the Imperial German Navy from the beginning of the 20th century. Admiral Alfred von Tirpitz had been appointed Navy Minister in 1897 and developed a deliberate long term strategy which saw the German Navy increase from 19 to 38 battle ships. Whilst it was still inferior to the Royal Navy it succeeded in posing a significant threat to Britain, who, due to the needs of her extensive Empire was never able to concentrate her full strength in the North Sea at any one time. Since the Napoleonic Wars, the Royal Navy had been relatively inactive in any major battles compared to the army which had been in action somewhere across the globe for all but one year of Queen Victoria's 64 year reign. By 1906, the technological advances at sea had resulted in the creation of the Dreadnought and with Britain possessing the greater number of ships, a colossal battle similar to that of Trafalgar had been envisaged by many naval strategists. The actions of the army and navy involved in epic battles had been officially recorded since the 18th century and these records quickly became part of a regiment's or ship's glorious history. In stark contrast, the actions of the Mercantile Marine often went unrecorded when operating in hazardous conditions whilst facing a continuous threat from mines and U-boats. With the belief that the war would be over by Christmas 1914, many fishermen joined the army, as did many miners and other key workers across the country, with so much valuable local knowledge and skills being lost. Realising this too late, the Government tried to bring many essential workers back before the Western Front claimed them terminally.

The mundane but essentially dangerous work carried out by thousands of Hull men along the East Coast and in the North Sea began from August 1914, after many mines had been laid by the German Navy in the early weeks of the war. The threat of mines had been recognised after the Russo-Japanese War 1904-05 and action was taken by the Royal Naval Volunteer Reserve to form a specialized section of trawlers for minesweeping duties. Despite this measure, it is unclear how seriously the possible implications of a U-boat war were taken in August 1914. The British trawler would go on to play an extremely effective dual role during the war by maintaining the provision of food stocks, whilst becoming involved in minesweeping and acting as armed vessels to counter the U-boat threat. Unlike the army, which drew new recruits from the civilian population, for the experienced seamen serving aboard armed trawlers and minesweepers, local knowledge and seamanship were essential skills passed down through generations of Hull families.

The landing of fish was affected very quickly, with many fish and chip shops forced to close whilst Hull's fishing industry went quickly into decline. By 1915, just 93 Hull trawlers were still engaged in fishing whilst more than 300 had been commandeered by the Admiralty. Along the East Coast the Scarborough fishing fleet was decimated very early on in the war, whilst Bridlington managed to carry on in what was considered by other port towns as a reviled practice of inshore trawling from motorised boats.

On 22nd August a German cruiser raid captured and sank eight trawlers, two of which were registered in Grimsby and six in Boston. From the 24-26th August, German vessels were engaged in laying mines along the East Coast. Between the Tyne and the Humber, some 16 trawlers were sunk by destroyers after the crews were taken prisoner. The Grimsby and North Sea Trawling fleet was badly affected with the *Rhine, Harrier, Lobelia, Seti, Valiant and Mersey* captured and sunk. A further six Grimsby Trawlers and four from Boston were also destroyed.

Thomas Jackson, a spare hand onboard the Hull trawler *'Imperialist'*, owned by Hellyer's, was an early Hull maritime casualty when the vessel hit a mine. His death on the 10th September left his widow and the mother of his two children prostrate with grief at their family home on John's Terrace, Walcott Street, Hull.

Almost 9,000 men from Hull and East Yorkshire served aboard 800 vessels. Around 670 trawlers were lost, more than 200 of them when engaged in minesweeping operations, accounting for the lives of over a thousand local men. A fleet of Grimsby trawlers spent five months clearing mines between Scarborough and Whitby from the end of 1914 until April 1915. During this time, around 70 mines were cleared although 4 minesweepers and 15 other vessels were lost, sometimes with as many as half the crews killed, although losses could often be much heavier. Charles Barnard was the only survivor from the Grimsby trawler Fitonia after she hit a mine on Sunday 6th September 1914.

Thomas Jackson, Hull trawler Imperialist Killed 10th September 1914

The Loss of HMS Aboukir, HMS Cressy, and HMS Hogue, 22 September 1914

The loss of the three cruisers was the first significant loss of life for Hull men serving with the Royal Navy during the war. Stalking the coast of Holland on 22nd September 1914 was the Unterseeboot U-9, commanded by Captain Otto Weddigen. His vessel was just a few metres below the surface lying in wait for unsuspecting British shipping. HMS *Aboukir*, HMS *Cressy* and HMS *Hogue* were armed cruisers built between 1899 and 1901 but due to the advance in naval technology, they were already becoming obsolete by 1914. On the morning of 22nd September 1914, HMS *Aboukir* was obliviously unaware of the presence of the U-9 and was the first to be hit when a torpedo was fired hitting her below the magazine, just after 6.00am. The *Hogue* and *Cressy* immediately came to the aid of their fatally damaged sister ship, although they were initially unaware of the cause of the impact. The *Hogue* came around to her port side, unclear whether a boiler had exploded or if she had hit a mine and whilst she was involved in despatching boats for the crew of the *Aboukir*, she too was hit by a torpedo. HMS *Aboukir* with her back broken, took around 30 minutes to sink, with some men able to come up on deck and get into lifeboats.

Hull Stoker, Robert Henry Walker, a father of four children, was killed onboard the Aboukir whilst A.B William Fagg, from 12, North Church Side in Hull survived. Able Seaman William Fagg's dramatic escape was told to the *Hull Daily Mail* when he arrived back in Hull for 10 days leave after the loss of the three cruisers.

Stoker Robert Henry Walker, killed on HMS Aboukir

Able Seaman William Fagg

HMS Aboukir

Hull Daily Mail September 1914

Mr William Fagg a former Boatswain on the S.S Brittania has had a miraculous escape from HMS Aboukir after it was hit by a torpedo. It was around six in the morning when the torpedo hit and Mr Fagg was asleep in his hammock after coming off watch at 04.30. He now has a scar and burns to his foot after his blanket was set ablaze. It took around half an hour for the Aboukir to sink giving those not killed or badly injured by the explosion time to get up on deck. Being a strong swimmer Fagg and other survivors swam with the tide towards the Hogue whilst those who could not swim boarded what boats were available. He was among 23 men picked up whilst five of the survivors later died. After being passed fit by the doctor at Chatham, Able Seaman William Fagg has returned to Hull looking fit and well after his ordeal with 10 days leave in front of him.

Despite William Fagg's dramatic escape, some 1,459 men were lost from the three cruisers, including several Hull men. Around 800 men were onboard the Aboukir when she went down, with 527 of them losing their lives. After the Hogue was hit whilst going to the aid of the stricken Aboukir, the Cressy immediately became aware that they were being targeted from below by U-Boats. She veered away, zig-zagging whilst firing her guns but she was the last of the cruisers to be hit in just under an hour.

Stoker Bursall, from Vauxhall Grove on Hessle Road and George Robert Thorpe were killed onboard HMS Cressy whilst Able Seamen Charles Hastings, William Pougher, Arthur Franklin, William Atkinson and Gunner Ernest Brumpton were Hull men killed onboard the Hogue after the vessel was the second to be hit. William Atkinson, a 41 year old former Reservist, had worked for Wilson's but rejoined the navy after 15 years on the reserve when war was declared. His death left a widow alone with their seven children on Waterloo Street in Hull. Arthur Franklin, a 34 year old naval Reservist had re-joined the navy just six weeks earlier when he was killed onboard HMS Hogue.

Arthur Franklin, killed on HMS Hogue 22 September 1914

Whilst it was not the first attack by German U-Boats on the Grand Fleet, it was the most devastating so far and clearly highlighted the deadly stealth and efficiency of the submarine. Just 820 survivors were rescued from around 2,280 men. The Kaiser displayed his pleasure at this deadly act by rewarding the Iron Cross to every member of the crew of the U-9. Germany's use of the submarine was having an immediate effect on the most powerful navy in the world. From November 1914, the Imperial German Navy declared the seas around Britain a War Zone with every Royal Naval and merchant vessel to be sunk on sight. The blockade of German ports by the Royal Navy was seen by Germany as giving them a moral and justifiable strategy, in what was becoming an increasingly bitter war of attrition.

The *Runo* was the first vessel of the Wilson Line to be sunk, one of 40 lost during the course of the war from the company, with a Board of Trade Inquiry taking place in January 1915. The losses in shipping in 1914 were down by around 800,000 tons compared to the previous year and by 1915 this had dropped even further, by one million, to 4,060,000 tons.

Ben Taylor, Hull, steward on the Runo

Built by Caledon Shipbuilding & Engineering at Dundee in 1902, in 1914 the Runo was owned by the Wilson Line, then the largest privately owned shipping company in the world. Whilst the majority of vessels built for the Wilson Line at the beginning of the 20th century came from Earle's Shipyard in Hull the Dundee Company had built the *Sappho, Salmo, Dago and Runo* between 1899-1902, two of which would be lost in the war. The *Runo*, a 1,650 ton cargo and passenger vessel was carrying 270 passengers and crew and a cargo of rubber when she hit a mine off the Tyne on Saturday 5th September at 16.30. Enroute to Archangel in Russia, the 280-foot *Runo*, a relatively large vessel for the time, was carrying nine lifeboats six of which were launched. Three later capsized due to overcrowding. Ben Taylor, a Hull steward on the *Runo* was one of 33 crew members. He helped to support an injured colleague alongside one of the upturned lifeboats for over two hours before being rescued. Hymns were sunk to keep up morale. The Hull Trawler *Cameo* was one of five ships to begin taking on survivors, with the *Runo* finally going down two hours later but not before twenty nine lives were lost. Frederick William Wollaston, skipper of the *Cameo*, was presented with a gold watch by the Lord Mayor of Hull on 1st October, whilst the five Hull and Grimsby skippers involved in rescuing survivors were awarded the Board of Trade silver medal for Bravery at Sea.

> *Four days after the loss of the Runo the Admiralty issued a press release which was carried in the Hull Daily Mail and other newspapers stating that "the Runo was sunk after diverting from Admiralty directions and had she not done so she would have had a safe journey". Admiralty instructions were uncompromising and strongly warned masters of the Mercantile Marine from straying from their recommended routes.*

The Runo passenger and cargo ship

The War will not be over by Christmas

By December 1914, it was apparent to all armies that the war would not be over by Christmas. The BEF had suffered around 90,000 casualties whilst the German Army had sustained around 700,000 and the French even more. Turkey's entry into the war in 1914 ensured that the boundaries would be stretched even further in 1915, with the European conflict developing into a global one. The war in 1914 was almost entirely confined to men serving in the army or navy prior to August 1914 or Reservists and some 20,000 Territorials, which ensured Hull's casualties were relatively light for the first five months of the conflict. Around 225 men were killed from across the city.

Whilst Hull men were serving in numerous regiments of the Regular army prior to August 1914, a significant portion of them involved in the first battles of the war were serving with the Coldstream Guards, which ensured that many of the first local casualties came from one of the three Guards battalions. (See appendix rear pages). Besides the loss of local men serving with the BEF, a significant number of Hull's first deaths were from men serving with the Royal Navy and Mercantile Marine.

By the end of December, over 1,185,330 men had volunteered from across Britain but it would be many months and even years before many of these men were ready for frontline service. Kitchener's New Armies, which included the four Hull Pals Battalions raised between August-November 1914, would not see service overseas until December 1915 and it would be March 1916 before they reached the Western Front. Like the Regular army, the Territorial Force had been mobilised in August 1914 but apart from the London Scottish and a few specialised units of engineers, signallers and artillery, they had not been required to serve overseas in significant numbers. With the BEF suffering casualties approaching more than 50 per cent during the first three months of war, by December the Territorials could no longer be kept out of the frontline or from Garrison duty overseas. This ensured 23 Battalions left for France in December whilst the 1/4th East Yorkshire Regiment a Territorial Battalion containing hundreds of Hull men, would leave for France in April 1915.

Christmas gift boxes sent to British troops in 1914, by 17 year old Princess Mary

Chapter Five

Please Come Quickly!

The East Yorkshire Regiment at the Second Battle of Ypres

The opening of 1915 saw stalemate along the Western Front, whilst new ways of killing and maiming were beginning to be used against both civilians and the military. HMS Formidable, a pre-dreadnought, was sunk in the English Channel on the 1st January with the loss of almost 550 officers and men. Zeppelin attacks had been anticipated and feared since the outbreak of war although none took place in 1914. Locally, there had been much anger and resentment at Hull Corporation after their decision to allow Hull Fair to be held during October 1914, whilst civilians and shop owners were being subjected to strict blackout regulations with heavy fines for those not complying. But it was not until January 1915 that Britain suffered its first Zeppelin raid, with Great Yarmouth being the first location hit, whilst Hull would be targeted for the first time in June.

The use of poison gas

Despite being banned by The Hague Convention of 1899, chlorine gas was used in January 1915, fired in artillery shells against the peasant armies of the Tsar. But it would be against the French at Ypres in April 1915 that its consequences proved almost disastrous for the allied lines, with two battalions of the East Yorkshire Regiment being some of those rushed up to fill the breech. After the use of chlorine gas, swift moral outrage followed at this most indiscriminate of weapons but it would soon be adopted as a weapon by all sides and used later in the year by the British Army at the French mining town of Loos, with near disastrous results for British troops as the wind changed. The use of chlorine and mustard gas increased as the war progressed, accounting for around 7 per cent of British casualties in 1917. By 1918 this had risen to 15 per cent.

With the 2nd Battalion East Yorkshire Regiment stationed in India for the duration of 1914, the 1st East Yorks was the only battalion from the regiment to see action on the Western Front during 1914. It was December when the second regular battalion of the East Yorkshire Regiment returned from Kamptee, bringing hundreds of experienced soldiers to France in January 1915. The further arrival of Territorials helped to free up Garrison troops for the front from across the Empire. The 1/4th East Yorkshire Regiment landed at Boulogne on 18th April with over 1,000 men whilst the 6th East Yorkshire Regiment, part of Kitchener's New Armies, who were also expecting to leave for France, travelled much further to Gallipoli.

British Troops prepared for a gas attack 1915

On 15th January, 26 officers and 968 men of the 2nd Battalion East Yorkshire Regiment sailed from Southampton onboard the SS City of Edinburgh, arriving the following day in Le Havre. They began disembarking at around 12.30, with men from the Kings Own Yorkshire Light Infantry. Both battalions had been posted to the 83rd Infantry Brigade 28th Division after returning from different parts of the Empire with the K.O.Y.L.I. arriving from Singapore in November. The freezing conditions of January and February 1915, with heavy snow falling, undoubtedly came as a harsh introduction to the Western Front for the East Yorkshire men after being accustomed to the Indian climate throughout 1914. After entraining at Le Havre, 2nd East Yorks left two platoons of around 100 men to follow on later and began a four hour journey to the Infantry Base Depot at Rouen, before arriving at Hazebrouck a small town in Northern France with strong Flemish roots but an important railway junction connecting it to the Channel Ports of Calais and Dunkirk.

With casualty clearing stations being established at Hazebrouck from October 1914 a hospital was already under construction and it was there, in the unfinished building that the battalion spent the night of 17th after being joined by the two platoons left behind in Le Havre. Between 17-27th the men built up their fitness by daily route marches, whilst undertaking trench relief.

On the morning of 28th January 1915, the 83rd Brigade paraded for Field Marshall Sir John French with 20 officers and 850 men of the 2nd East Yorks presenting themselves for inspection. On the 29th, the 28th Division moved to relieve a French Division after being transported by motor bus to Vlamertinghe. From there they marched to Ypres on the 1st February, were along with other Yorkshiremen from the K.O.Y.L.I, they took over the trenches from the French 62nd Brigade very near to the Ypres-Comines Canal. The 2nd East Yorks moved several times during February and March as they were relieved or moved back into the frontline, with units taking over various sections of the Houplines Sector. Regimental War Diaries vary considerably. Some record obscure and interesting facts, such as the number of dug outs, and the weather, whilst others, often written in appalling handwriting and in terrible conditions, hold less detail and simply state military action and casualties. What they all have in common is the recording of heavy shelling, often on a daily basis, sometimes lasting for an hour and on other occasions going on all day, causing heavy casualties and damage in the trenches. Just days after the battalion had arrived at Ypres, the Germans launched an early morning attack with "B" Company being driven from a portion of the trench and losing the battalion's two Vickers machine guns in the process, whilst the following day Lieutenant Oscar James Addyman was killed instantly and Captain Osborn Cecil Wilkinson seriously wounded by the same shell. He

British troops arriving at Le Havre, 1914

later died from his wounds. Casualties throughout February were heavy, with 73 men killed and 132 were missing, 5 officers had been killed and 5 wounded, accounting for over 20 per cent of the battalion and more than one third of its officers. With the continual development of the expanding trench network system in 1915, much of the time was spent digging new communication trenches, which were essential for moving troops and supplies to and from the frontline in relative safety. The Battalion War Diary for March tells of quiet days which allowed a company of 250 men to be detailed for trench digging, with intermittent shelling causing a few casualties. The casualty figures for March were in double figures- 2 officers and 11 other ranks killed and 50 wounded.

One of the two officers killed in March was 2nd Lieutenant Henry Drummond Payne from Hull, he died from wounds to the pelvis at Battalion Headquarters at "Tea Farm." He was laid to rest in the local churchyard at Dranoutre at nine in the evening to avoid enemy artillery. On the 7th April the 2nd East Yorks were inspected by General Sir Horace Smith- Dorrien a veteran of the Zulu War and one of just a handful of men to escape from the disastrous battle of Isandlwana in January 1879. The following day, motor buses transported the men to Ypres and from there they moved to Zonnebeke, where they took over trenches previously occupied by the French and found them to be in a desperate condition; too shallow and filled with water, they afforded very little protection. During March the battalion became attached to the 5th Division for the month, before resuming their role with the 28th Division during April. Most of April passed by uneventfully with a few casualties sustained and the men resting in hutments behind the lines.

2nd Lieutenant. Henry Drummond Payne died of wounds

The Second Battle of Ypres, 22 April-25 May 1915

On the 22nd April the orders came for the 2nd Battalion East Yorkshire Regiment to "stand to" after the Germans had broken through and were occupying parts of the French line near St Julien. The second battle for control of the medieval cloth town of Leper, known as the Second Battle of Ypres had already begun and would last for over a month, encompassing four battles.

The 2nd East Yorks had suffered hundreds of casualties in the past three months, (over 200 alone in February) and had a fighting strength of less than 650, when they were ordered to attack alongside the York & Lancs Regiment, whilst being under the command of Lieutenant Colonel A. D Geddes of the "Buffs". The action of Friday 23rd began at 4.10pm, with the East Yorks advancing towards the German trenches some 1,500 yards away. Although the attack got within 30 yards of the German wire the enemy fire had caused very heavy casualties, leaving an already depleted battalion incapable of securing and holding any section of the German line. They were then ordered to retire. A small party under Corporal Hall failed to hear the order to retire and became stranded 30 yards from the German trenches. Without any food or water, it was two days later before the men were able to withdraw under cover of darkness to their own trenches.

Officers- Killed	wounded	missing
4	9	1

other ranks- killed	wounded	missing
42	256	72

After some of the wounded had been brought in under the cover of darkness, less than 300 men, (under half the battalion that set out), went into reserve trenches. With so many wounded and missing and men later dying from wounds during the coming weeks, the true casualties of Friday 23rd April may never be fully known, whilst most of the men posted as missing were believed to have been killed. The Battalion War Diary proudly states that this attack was instrumental in checking the German advance, whilst saving the town of Ypres from falling into German hands as it allowed vital reinforcements to be brought up at a critical time. Exhausted and with their numbers devastated the survivors of the battalion were resting in hutments at the end of April when they received a draft of 10 officers and 63 other ranks. Despite being in reserve to the Canadian Division at Polygon Wood they were subjected to a murderous seven hour barrage on the 5th May, losing 35 men and suffering over 170 casualties. It is difficult to disguise the failure of the British artillery at this time. They had been supplied with too few shells of poor quality. The German artillery was utterly dominant in the spring of 1915,

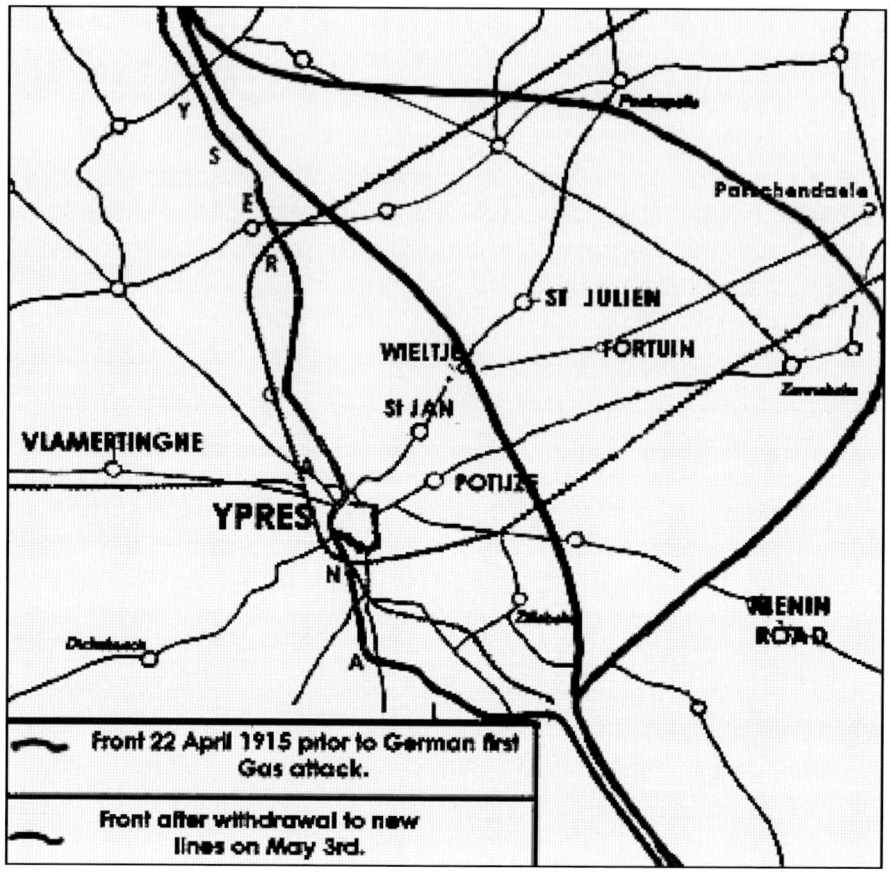

causing very heavy casualties whilst having limitless rounds. This was responsible for the abandonment of a planned attack on the 9th May. Several days later the failure of the quality and quantity of British shells would be exposed in the Daily Mail causing a national scandal the "shell crisis". This resulted in the fall of the Liberal Government, although Asquith remained as Prime Minister, whilst a cross party coalition was put in to place which included a new Cabinet of 12 Liberals, 8 Conservatives, and 1 Labour minister. Shell production then came under the control of a national body, the Ministry of Munitions, headed by David Lloyd George.

The 9th May was another day of heavy bombardment for the East Yorkshire men, leaving them impotent with no water, their telephone lines cut and no communication trenches preventing the wounded from being evacuated. Before reinforcements were received the battalion was left with just 5 officers and 283 other ranks, a shadow of its former self. A much needed draft of 406 officers and other ranks joined on the 15th May over 350 of them volunteers from the Staffordshire Regiment and by the time the battalion was inspected by the Commander–in-Chief Field Marshall Sir John French, their numbers had swollen to 14 officers and 837 other ranks. The Second Battle of Ypres ended on the 25th May causing the 2nd East Yorks the following casualties, whilst the British Army suffered some 59,000 casualties.

Officers				Other Ranks		
Killed	Wounded	Missing		Killed	Wounded	Missing
4	9	1		87	451	99

Lieutenant Colonel Walter Herbert Young arrived in May and took over command. On 31st May the adjutant recorded the following casualties in the Battalion War Diary which included all those killed, injured and missing since the battalion had arrived in France on 16th January 1915.

Officers				Other Ranks		
Killed	Wounded	Missing		Killed	Wounded	Missing
11	38	1		189	675	117

In just 19 weeks, the 2nd East Yorks had suffered some 1,031 casualties, making an average of 54 casualties per week. The crucial role played by the 2nd East Yorks and the entire 28th Division was expressed on the 21st May in a telegram from the Commander in Chief, Field Marshal Sir John French. "It is with thanks and deep appreciation to every officer, NCO, and man, for their splendid work, bravery and magnificent fighting qualities in the recent severe fighting around the Ypres salient (Second Battle of Ypres)".

Hull Territorials leave for the Front

Nine hours after the 2nd East Yorks had attacked and suffered very heavy casualties at the Second Battle of Ypres, the Hull Territorials were ordered into their first action of the war on Saturday 24th April, just six days after arriving in France.

The creation of the Territorial Force in 1908 replaced local militia and volunteer units. Each Territorial unit became responsible for the defence of a particular area or section of the British coastline. Up until the Military Service Act of 1916, men would not be compelled to serve overseas unless they volunteered to do so.

Despite Kitchener's reservations and lack of confidence in the Territorial Force, many thousands had left for France and Flanders by December 1914, whilst 50,000 set sail for India and Egypt to free up regular battalions for the Western Front. The 4th and 5th East Yorks were Territorial battalions, with the 5th being made up of many Hull cyclists. Commanded by Sir Robert Aske, they were retained for coastal defence throughout the duration of the war. Lord Kitchener, Secretary of State for War, who had forged his reputation in the Sudan and South Africa, viewed the recently formed Territorial Force with a good deal of disdain. The part-time role and what he saw as inadequate training undertaken by many office clerks, bank managers and company directors at weekends undoubtedly prejudiced his feelings. Worried about home defence, he realised from the outbreak of war that the Territorials would be required to provide a vital role, whether it be at home or overseas. Going against the popular opinion that the war would be over by Christmas, Kitchener advised the War Cabinet in August that sea power alone would not be sufficient and that millions of men would be required in the field for at least three years. His very realistic prediction turned out to be highly accurate in terms of men required and the longevity of the war. This may have been influenced by his experiences in South Africa, when it had taken the British Empire over two years and 450,000 troops to subdue less than 50,000 highly mobile Afrikaners.

In August 1914, the Territorial Force was mobilised just after many battalions had returned or were ordered to return from their annual summer camps. The 4th East Yorks were in North Wales when they were suddenly ordered back to Londesborough Barracks in Hull at the end of July. On the 29th July six days before the declaration of war, Territorial units were already preparing for possible military action with a Special Service Section of two officers and 50 men arriving in Hull, where bayonets were sharpened and ammunition collected. Some 680 men were mustered at Londesborough Barracks before the battalion marched off to billets in Hedon, where they received a further 133 recruits. By the 11th August the battalion, which had a strength of 26 officers and 913 other ranks, moved to Darlington, where training began. Territorials were not forced to serve overseas unless they volunteered to do so but this they did in overwhelming numbers. With the sudden movement of thousands of troops across the country, accommodating men was a logistical problem for many communities with public buildings such as schools and halls being commandeered. Some of the 4th East Yorks where billeted in Corporation schools across Darlington, whilst 400 men left to erect tents at Hummersknott Park, near the Town's waterworks. It was at this time that volunteers were called for to serve overseas as a separate unit, with 75 per cent volunteering for Imperial Service, whilst Lieutenant Colonel Shaw went to Hull, where he secured the services of over 350 men who agreed to serve overseas should they be required to. On the 14th September, the battalion was divided between Foreign and Home Service men, with 150 men who had volunteered for Home Service returning to Hull in October whilst 121 new recruits from Hull took their place. Across Darlington and Newcastle men were undergoing rigorous training, some of which involved entraining with horses, whilst the first inoculations were taking place for Foreign Service men.

Lieutenant Colonel George Hubert Shaw Commanding 1/4th East Yorks

The build up of men in such close proximity ensured a perfect breeding ground for lice with all army kit and blankets being moved to the local workhouse. Lord Nunburnholme, the architect of the Hull Pals, came up to visit the Yorkshiremen in December 1914 and by January 1915 the 4th East Yorks numbered 31 officers, 52 sergeants, 16 drummers and 908 other ranks whilst 53 horses were in their possession. During the course of the war, almost 700 battalions were raised by the Territorial Force with over 300 battalions seeing overseas service. Small, specialised units of signallers and artillery belonging to the Territorial Force did serve on the Western Front in 1914 but it was not until 1915 that their numbers were brought to the front in significant strength, with the 1/4th East Yorks arriving in France on the 18th April.

Hull Businessmen Commanding the 1/4th East Yorks

Had the 1st Hull Pals not been un-officially known as the "Commercials," then the 1/ 4th East Yorks would have undoubtedly taken the title, due to the number of prominent Hull businessmen serving as officers within the battalion. The officers of the battalion mostly came from the traditional upper middle classes who were employed in senior roles in local industry, with all of them known to each other. Captain Cecil Ingleby was the nephew of George Hubert Shaw, the Commanding Officer of 4th East Yorks. Shaw's military career began back in 1883 as a 19 year old, when he joined the ranks and a year later he gained a commission. Regular promotion followed as he combined his commercial life with his military service. Almost 50 years of age in 1914, Shaw was a wealthy malting & barley merchant, (Shaw & Sons), with premises on High Street, where he employed John Jackson, a sergeant in the battalion as a clerk. In an attempt to improve his wife's health, Shaw moved his family to Hornsea and had four grown up sons by 1914, one serving in France whilst two were engaged in fruit farming in British Columbia. Shaw took over command of the 1/ 4th East Yorks in 1910 from W Hall.

Major Carl Eric Theilmann

In command of "B" Company was 41 year old Major Carl Eric Theilmann. The son of a Danish corn merchant, he was head of Theilmann & Son Corn and Seed Merchants and lived at 90, Westbourne Avenue in 1914 with his wife and two young children. Besides being a successful merchant, Theilmann was also a distinguished linguist, involved in interpreting and marking German language examination papers. Living at 153, Westbourne Avenue was another Territorial officer, Major Herman Gosschalk. He was the son of a Dutch merchant. The tight knit group of local officers living along the wealthy Avenues area in West Hull is further demonstrated by James Rishworth, living on Park Avenue; he was the Managing Director of the Swan Flour Mill and another Territorial officer.

Bede Farrell, an Old Hymerian, was an experienced officer serving with the battalion. For over a decade he combined a legal career with his military duties. After completing a course in Militia and Infantry Training at Chelsea Barracks, he was offered a commission in the regular army in 1901, which he turned down to pursue his legal studies. On passing the Law Society's final examination and gaining a Second Class Honours Degree in 1904 he was articled to his father, a solicitor in the Hull firm Rollit & Co. Working as a Hull solicitor, he served as a lieutenant and then a captain alongside his younger brother in the 1st Volunteer Battalion East Yorkshire Regiment. In 1908, when the Volunteer Units were replaced by the Territorial Force, Farrell continued to serve, becoming a senior captain and acting adjutant. At the outbreak of war he volunteered for overseas service.

Captain Bede Farrell

Sidney Hannaford Hellyer was the 25 year old son of Charles Hellyer, owner of the Steam Fishing Co Ltd, a hugely successful Hull trawling company. Living on Newland Park, Cottingham Road, he had previously been a former cadet at Malvern College. In August 1914, he joined the Territorial Force and was gazetted 2nd lieutenant in the 1/4th East Yorkshire Regiment in September 1914.

It was these Hull men and others from across East Yorkshire who would lead the companies and platoons of the 1/4th East Yorks at the Second Battle of Ypres. Amongst the Hull officers commanding the 1/4th were the Farrell and Easton brothers. Of the four men, only Arthur Easton would survive the war. For some, their first action of the war would be their last as the battalion suffered heavy casualties, (particularly amongst its officers), throughout April and May. George Hubert Shaw, the Battalion Commander of the 1/4th East Yorks, took the Territorials to France onboard the RMS Invicta on 17th April. The battalion was divided into four companies. Captain Farrell commanded "A" company, Major Theilmann "B", Captain Robson "C", and Captain Morrill "D", with each of the companies comprising 250 men. Two officers were left back in England for training purposes, whilst 29 officers and 1,023 other ranks arrived at Boulogne on Sunday morning 18th April. The 4th East Yorks belonged to the 50th Northumbrian Division, 150th Infantry Brigade, which comprised of 4th Yorks, 5th Yorks Regiment and the 5th Durham Light Infantry, commanded by Brigadier-General J.E Bush.

Sidney Hannaford Hellyer, with his mother Jane Victoria Hannford, Lambwath Hall Sutton,

After disembarking around midday on Sunday 18th, the battalion marched off to Pont de Briques and entrained for Bavinchore Station at Cassel, where they were billeted for the night. The following day they had reached the outskirts of Steenvoorde with the men settling into billets on and around local farms, whilst the battalion headquarters were established in the Callicanni Inn, with a telephone line connecting them to Brigade Headquarters at Chateau-de-la-Bean.

Whilst most of the battalion's officers were preparing for the first military action of their careers, NCO's like Sergeant John Jackson, who had been working as a clerk for George H. Shaw in 1914, had years of military experience. Living and working on High Street in Hull, Jackson had served 21 years with 2nd Battalion East Yorkshire Regiment, seeing active service during the Boer War. On leaving the Regular army, Jackson joined the Territorials in 1912 and volunteered for overseas service in 1914.

In comparison to many battalions the 4th East Yorks had only a very short time to prepare. After arriving at Boulogne they had just six days before their first action of the war. A direct consequence of the first gas attack on the Western Front at Langermarck was the battalion's premature entry into the frontline during the Second Battle of Ypres. After 170 tons of chlorine gas had been released across a five mile front, French colonial and Territorial troops became overwhelmed, abandoning their trenches in a desperate panic. This created a gap of about a mile in the Allied line with the Germans pushing forward to occupy parts of the Yser Canal. After the first gas attack on Thursday 22nd April, the village of St Julien, which had been to the rear of the 1st Canadian Division, was then left in the frontline, leaving it vulnerable to a flank attack. Chlorine gas acts as a severe irritant, attacking the respiratory system and affecting the eyes, throat and lungs.

After an order by a Canadian Medical Officer, a former industrial chemist, the Colonial troops were ordered to urinate into cloths and handkerchiefs and hold them to their airways for protection against the poisonous fumes. The 150th Brigade was ordered to move within 24 hours of the attack. Just four days after disembarking at Boulogne the Territorials received unexpected orders to concentrate at Battalion Headquarters. The men would have been aware that there was something in the offing, with 40 London motor buses arriving to transport the 1,000 men to Poperinghe, from where they marched to wooden hutments at the village of Vlamertinghe with the boom of the guns growing louder.

Sgt. John Jackson, Boer War Veteran, killed 3rd May 1915

The Battle of St Julien
24th April-4th May 1915

The 1/4th East Yorks were awoken and stood to at 01.30 on the morning of Saturday 24th, before marching off to occupy and hold trenches along the Yser Canal, where they came under artillery fire. Although no men were killed during this time, several men were wounded, becoming the battalion's first casualties of the Great War. Later in the morning, the East Yorkshire men were ordered to make a counter attack, with the Canadians on their right and other battalions, including the Green Howards, it began just before 4.00pm.

In a letter home to his grandfather, written two days after the battle, 2nd Lieutenant Sidney Hellyer has left us with a very frank and descriptive account of the action involving the 4th East Yorks on the 24th. His status as a junior officer undoubtedly helped to ensure that his letter was not subjected to the same censorship as that of non commissioned officers and describes the deaths of three of the battalion's senior officers.

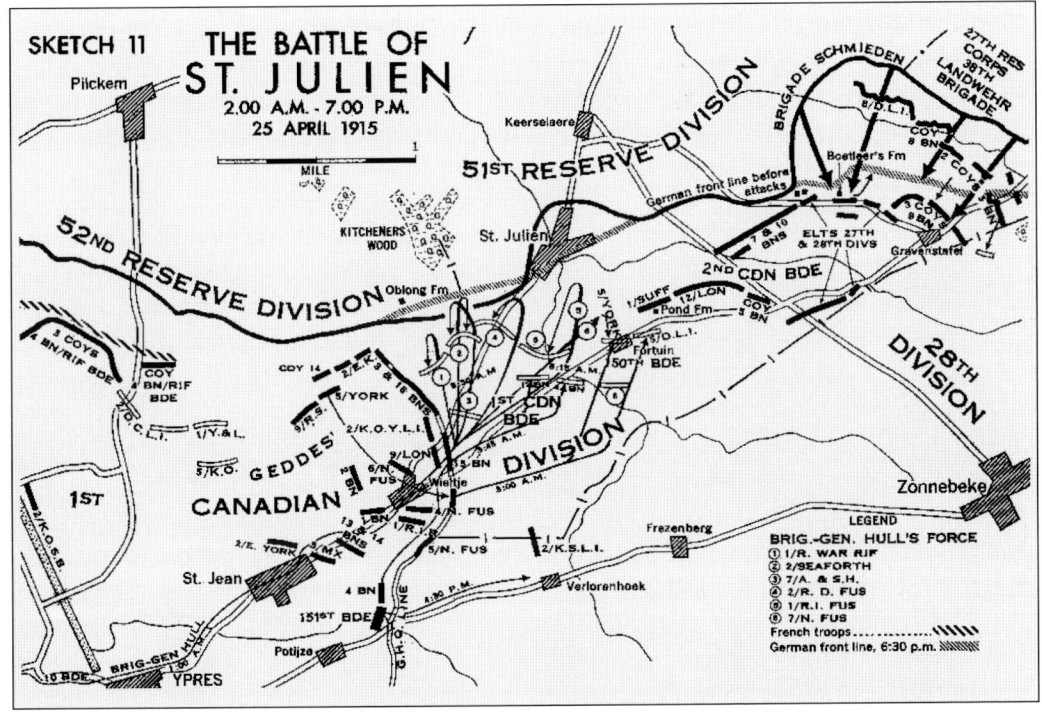

The Second Battle of Ypres

Around 4 o'clock on the afternoon of (Saturday 24th April) for the first time in the history of the battalion, and what a bloody battle it was. We advanced in artillery formation across half a mile of open countryside and under heavy bombardment, both of shrapnel and high explosive shells, and many men fell absolutely heroically there is no other word for it. I would never have believed hardened men would have marched on under that bombardment, and these men already very tired, having two sleepless nights, having carrying loads of 70lbs since we left Newcastle and hardly having their boots off since that time, saw battle for the first time as if they were going to the barbers for a barbers shave. Three times within 20 minutes a shell struck the ground near the men I have the honour to lead, once within 10 yards and when the high explosive shells they dive into the earth and the end of the world seems to have come. They blow a hole the size of the pond in the back field at Lambwath, and the contents of the hole are blown into the sky, much higher than a trawlers mast, so high that one has to lie on one's face that seems like 20 seconds until all the earth and fragments have fallen. When one strikes near, one is covered with earth, so that there is difficulty rising under the weight of it. The noise deafens and stuns one. One shell blew us down in a body without killing any of us. This bombardment went on incessantly, not a shell now and then, but all the shells bursting, sometimes two or three hitting the same spot at once. After the third time we were covered in earth and a man of mine shouted to me; if these B__s don't ring the bell soon we go and give them their money back. After advancing for 20 minutes, the high explosive shells ceased, and we went into the zone of rifle and machine-gun fire still in daylight and over fallow land. They never worried a bit, never faltered, never laid down to the shrapnel a moment longer than was necessary. Col Shaw was shot dead at this stage. My Captain, Bede Farrell was shot through the heart a minute or two later. Major Theilmann met instant death, and a man who went to help him was shot dead as he rose. When we reached the village, advancing in rushes with fixed bayonets, the Germans fell back without waiting for our assault. We collected our men, and carried what poor fellows we could and marched the remainder back to some trenches about 500 yards to the rear of our position.

George Hubert Shaw would be the second battalion commander of the East Yorkshire Regiment to be killed in his first action of the war and the first in 1915 but not the last. Within a few deadly minutes, three senior officers from the battalion had been killed. This left the C.O and two out of four company commanders dead, whilst the Battalion War Diary states 3 officers and 12 other ranks were killed, 76 were wounded and 7 were missing, accounting for 10 per cent of the battalion. Exhausted and soaked through, the battalion took cover in shallow trenches during the night of the 24th. On the morning of the 25th, the battalion marched off to empty trenches more than a mile away. Seeing that the trenches were unoccupied, the Germans shelled them heavily with Lieutenant Frank Grindell, from Norfolk Street in Hull and five men being buried alive, before they were eventually dragged out wounded and bruised. After marching at night, the battalion suffered further casualties to shrapnel.

The Death of Sidney Hannaford Hellyer

Born on 15th August 1889, Sidney Hannaford Hellyer was sent to away to be educated at St John the Evangelist, School in Eastbourne. By 1911, he was a director and partner in the Hull family firm of Hellyer's Steam Fishing Company, with his father Charles Hellyer, a native of Brixham. Being one of Hull's most successful ship owners responsible for providing an essential role in supporting local industry and the Home Front, it is almost certain that Sidney Hannaford Hellyer would have been exempt from any military service throughout the duration of the war.

But 18 months before the introduction of conscription and just weeks after the declaration of war, he enlisted in the Territorial Force, joining the 1/ 4th East Yorks. He was gazetted 2nd Lieutenant in the Machine Gun Section on 12th September 1914. Like so many officers of the battalion Sidney Hellyer's overseas service was very short. Just 11 days after disembarking at Boulogne he received the fatal wounds which led to his death 10 days later. Four days after the action of 24th April which had claimed the lives of three of the battalion's senior officers, 2nd Lieutenant Sidney Hannaford Hellyer was ordered to take his platoon and entrench between the canal and Pilkem Road. On the afternoon of Wednesday 28th April, whilst overseeing his men digging in nearer to the German lines a shrapnel shell burst in the midst of their party, killing five instantly and wounding eleven others, including 2nd Lieutenant Sidney Hellyer. Despite his severe injuries, which included his arm being blown off at the shoulder and wounds to the legs, his remaining arm and his face, he insisted the other injured men were treated before he was attended to. From their exposed position, he was carried with great courage by stretcher bearers of the Royal Army Medical Corps to a trench ambulance. Hellyer and the other injured men would probably have been transported by a horse- drawn field ambulance, as they could often get closer to the trenches and then moved to a dressing station, from where they would be moved to the railhead by motor ambulance. During darkness, the ambulance lost its way and all the two orderlies could do to stem the blood loss was to press their muddy fingers and thumbs into his open wounds. Incredibly, he survived to be transported to the Base Hospital in Boulogne, from where he had entered the war just days earlier. But within a couple of days, his wounds would have begun to fester, when the smell of gangrene began to permeate the air. He lingered for another ten days and was able to dictate letters home to his parents at Lambwath Hall, Sutton, reassuring them that his wounds were light and that he would be seeing them soon. No word of his grievous injuries or of the pain he was enduring was expressed in any of his letters, before he succumbed to his wounds on Saturday 8th May 1915, at No 7 Stationary Hospital, Boulogne.

Sergeant Thomas Hurd of "A" Company was one of several from the battalion who paid tribute to Hellyer's extreme bravery, stating that he was extremely popular with all officers and men. His body was returned to England where he was buried in Brixham, Devon, the birthplace of his father and grandfather. The Hellyer family was hit by further tragic news just days later when George Peabody Hellyer, from Kirk Ella also died from his wounds. Born in the same year as his cousin Sidney, he was also serving with a Territorial battalion, 1/5th King's Liverpool Regiment and died just 13 days later.

Brixham, Devon the resting place of Sidney Hellyer

*Hull Ship's Chandler,
Captain. Bernard Marshall Sharp*

*Captain Charles Harland Judge,
died of wounds 17th May*

The heavy German artillery and the newly dug trenches were a significant factor in causing so many casualties amongst the battalion in the coming days and weeks. After being directed to trenches which were already occupied the battalion went into reserve trenches, which were vulnerable to shelling. They were immediately targeted by German artillery. Bernard Marshall Sharp, a 32 year old partner in E.E Sharp and Sons on High Street was one of 11 men injured by shrapnel on 30th April. He was sent back to England to recover from his wounds, returning in to the front in June with 14 other ranks.

The following three days were ones of heavy shelling, with 10 men killed on the 1st May whilst Captain Charles Harland Judge, a Machine Gun Officer from Hull and 13 other ranks were wounded.

As with many men injured in 1914-15, Captain Judge's immediate wounds were not serious enough to take his life. After being taken to a Regimental Aid Post, he would have been transported by ambulance to a casualty clearing station and finally by rail to the Base Hospital in Boulogne. Like Sidney Hellyer, he was able to write home to his parents at 107, Park Avenue in Hull, before dying from his wounds some 17 days later. The thick clay mud of Flanders so often became embedded in wounds at the moment of impact, with infection quickly setting in, eventually claiming the lives of men who just two years later would have survived similar injuries due to advances in medical treatment which included blood transfusions.

Between the 1st and 3rd May the battalion hung on in the trenches despite being subjected to an almost continuous heavy bombardment which claimed the life of another officer from Park Avenue, Lieutenant James Rishworth, the Managing Director of a Hull flourmill. A further six officers were wounded with two later dying of wounds. Monday 3rd May was a particularly black day for Hull men, (as would prove to be the same date in May 1917 for local men serving with the East Yorkshire Regiment). The Battalion Diary records the deaths of 22 on the 3rd, whilst 33 were killed between the 1-3rd May and 59 wounded, almost all Hull men. Under the cover of a heavy artillery barrage the Germans attacked what had become a vulnerable part of the line but were eventually driven back with very heavy casualties. Before retiring to Pottenhoek, under the cover of darkness the day's dead were buried and the wounded transported to dressing stations. Charles Blyth from Colonial Street, William Norton of Somerset Street, Arthur Hilton of Great Thornton Street, Thomas Kidd, of Hawthorn Avenue, Thomas Devine of Walker Street, John Jackson of High Street, Lawrence Mitchell from Francis Street and James Rishworth were just some of the 22 Hull men killed or dying of wounds received on 3rd May. With so many wounded men, the deaths of the 3rd May rose from the 22 recorded that day by the Battalion War Diary. From 24th April-3rd May, the battalion had lost many experienced men with seven officers, three sergeants, and a company sergeant major, all from Hull being killed or later dying from wounds. [See appendix rear pages].

Sgt. 1062 Arthur Hilton, one of 22 Hull men killed on 3rd May 1915

When the battalion went into General Reserve for five days on the 4th May, 18 out of 29 officers had become casualties, 10 of them Hull men, it had a fighting strength of 621 other ranks. The Second Battle of Ypres was the most costly action of the war for Hull men, (up until that time) with both 2nd East Yorks and the 1/4th East Yorks suffering heavy casualties after going into action just hours apart from each other in an attempt to hold the line leading to the medieval but strategically vital town of Ypres. During the coming days, the losses were devastating for the Hull Territorials 33 were killed between 1-3rd May, almost all local men and by the end of May, over 75 officers and men from the city had lost their lives. Wounded men such as Lieutenant Frank Norman Saxelbye, from Park Avenue, (who had worked for the British Oil and Coke Co as a travelling salesman), would later die of their wounds in the Base Hospital at Boulogne. The 2nd East Yorks, who had attacked just hours before the Territorials, had suffered even greater casualties at Ypres and had been reduced to less than 300 men by 9th May.

The shock and outpouring of grief and patriotic pride from across the city was extremely evident in the two local papers, the Hull Daily Mail and Hull Daily News, with several whole pages displaying the photographs of those killed, wounded and serving with the "Glorious 4th" as they were being called. Up until the spring of 1915, the deaths of Hull men on any one day had usually been in single figures, but never on such a scale as those suffered by the city during the Second Battle of Ypres. Letters from wounded officers like Major Arthur Easton tell of the heroic death of Lieutenant Colonel Shaw and Major Theilmann and of the devastation all around them, which he labeled "the city of dead". Drummer R. Risdale of "A" company wrote about the particular sadness of his own Company Commander's death. Captain Bede Farrell was shot through the heart whilst leading from the front. Several of the letters from Hull men to their families tell of their miraculous survival, some of whom would be killed just days and weeks later. Archibald Amos wrote to his sister on Tynemouth Street in Hull, delighted with the box of Capstans that she had just sent him and describing how he had escaped the terrific bombardment of the 3rd with just his precious carton of cigs still intact. However he would be killed just two weeks later on the 24th May. Whilst the overwhelming numbers of casualties in April and May serving with 1/4th East Yorks were Hull men, there were others from two of East Yorkshires largest towns, Beverley and Bridlington. Reckitts had numerous employees serving with the 1/4th, with Walter Stanley Murray, a former employee, being tragically killed by Private Chester whilst cleaning his rifle, when a negligent discharge occurred on the 11th June. With the senior officer ranks decimated Lieutenant Colonel H.R Beddoes of the Dublin Fusiliers arrived on the 12th May and took over command. By the end of the month, the battalion numbered 19 officers and 490 other ranks, whilst 149 men who had not been evacuated to England were in the Base Hospital. The Territorials were unfortunate in being moved to many sectors of the line during the Second Battle of Ypres, coming under the command of several different divisions including the 1st and 3rd Calvary Divisions. Charles Woodcock, a corporal with the 1/4th, told the Hull Daily Mail that the Territorials fighting qualities at the Second Battle of Ypres had gained them a degree of respect from the battle hardened Canadians, who had nicknamed them "The Mad Mullahs".

The 1st Canadian Division, which was made up of lumberjacks, farmers and businessmen, staged a stubborn and determined defence at Ypres in their first major engagement of the war. This was crucial in holding up the German offensive, allowing the British Army time to bring troops, including the two battalions of the East Yorkshire Regiment, into the line. The Ypres Salient, which was vulnerable to attack from three sides, would be held by the British throughout the duration of the war and was always under attack because of its strategic importance, which denied the Germans access to the English Channel. Whilst the allied lines held at Ypres, the ground between the German lines and the town had been reduced, making it more vulnerable to shelling. With a major battle taking place for its capture in every year of the war except 1916, the medieval streets and squares of the town were reduced to rubble whilst the defence of Ypres would become a symbol of continued endurance.

The Second Battle of Ypres had cost the Germans over 34,000 casualties whilst Allied losses were more than double, with the Canadian's suffering 6,000 in their first major action. British casualties were over 59,000, with chlorine gas claiming the lives of over 300 men. The French suffered 18,000 casualties whilst Hull's losses were hundreds of men killed, wounded, and missing from the two East Yorkshire Battalions.

Reduced to rubble, the medieval cloth town of Leper
The City of the dead where nothing lives but starving barking dogs"
Major Arthur Easton, 1/4th East Yorks Second Battle of Ypres

Chapter Six

Distant Guns;
The 6th East Yorks sail for Gallipoli July 1915

Regarded as the sick man of Europe, Britain and France had fought a war on the fringes of Europe just 60 years earlier in the Crimea, to prevent Russian expansion and prop up the ailing Ottoman Empire. Despite the Turkish army being trained and reorganized by the German General Liman Von Sanders, from the early years of the 20th century Turkey was still regarded as a secondary enemy after their entry into the war on the side of Germany in 1914. Whilst a successful Allied campaign would have knocked Turkey out of the conflict, the war still had to be won on the Western Front.

Betrayed by poor intelligence and inadequate planning

From the outset, the Dardanelles campaign was marred by a mixture of poor intelligence, inadequate naval preparations and missed opportunities. Intelligence, good maps, and local knowledge are essential for any military campaign to be successful, especially an amphibious invasion thousands of miles from Britain. One man, Colonel Cunliffe-Owen, had intimate pre-war knowledge of the terrain, of the location of Turkish gun en-placements and the geographical layout of the Gallipoli peninsula which had enabled him to make detailed surveys in 1914. Despite his precise knowledge he was not consulted by the War Office nor was he was part of a group of staff officers who were hastily put together, ensuring that his valuable reports did not reach General Sir Ian Hamilton and the high command. The chance to destroy the obsolete and poorly manned Turkish defences at the Dardanelles and open up a supply route to Russia thus knocking Turkey out of the war, was missed in 1914 by a mixture of short-sightedness and indecisiveness by both the British and Russians. After opening up a second front, the eight month campaign was hampered by a series of blunders and failed opportunities, drawing in over 410,000 British and Empire troops.

The Gallipoli peninsula was probably the most compact of all the Great War battlefield arenas, stretching for around 40 miles in length and about 12 miles across at its widest point. The geographical features of this area, the arid valleys, gulleys, ravines and hills made it an area of serene but rugged beauty in the summer but one of natural defence. If the opposing trenches of the Western Front were in close proximity, then those on Gallipoli were even closer, often less than 10 yards apart, allowing improvised bombs made from jam jars to be thrown

The cramped dugouts and bridgeheads at Gallipoli

into the Turkish trenches. With extremes of weather, from the scorching heat of the summer to thousands of men going down with frost bite in early December, the terrain and climate could be as much of a weapon as enemy action, with thousands of men suffering from dysentery. Almost 3,000 miles from Dover to Cape Helles, nobody that went to Gallipoli ever came home on leave, whilst the sick and wounded were evacuated to the island of Lemnos. The failed Gallipoli campaign which was played out under the clear blue skies of the Aegean is often thought of as something of a Greek Tragedy. The Romantic Poet, Rupert Brooke, immortalized the feelings of men dying in foreign lands in his most famous poem "The Soldier", written in 1914 for those men serving in France and Flanders. Today Rupert Brooke is very much associated with Gallipoli but his death from sepsis (blood poisoning) came before he ever reached the sandy shores and rugged terrain of the peninsula.

If I should die, think only this of me:
That there is some corner of a foreign field that is forever England
There shall be in that rich earth concealed; a dust whom
England bore shaped made aware

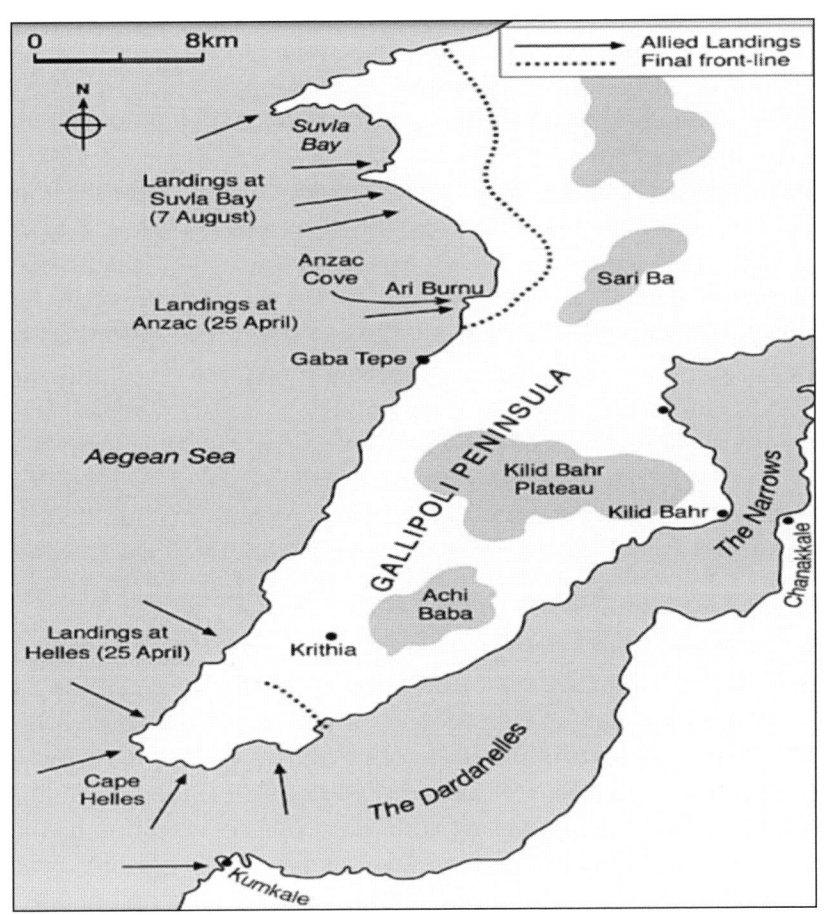

Gallipoli was where the blood of young nations, Australia and New Zealand (the ANZACS) would be spilt and where so much had been invested and expected, particularly by Winston Churchill, Lord of the Admiralty, who would later be dismissed by Prime Minister Asquith.

The 6th East Yorkshire Regiment, part of Kitchener's New Armies, was raised at Beverley in August 1914. By the end of the month, the battalion had reached full strength. In December 1914, the 6th East Yorks were billeted at Grantham, when they officially became the Pioneer Battalion for the 11th Northern Division. Belonging to a northern division, the 6th East Yorks contained a rich diversity of northern men from Hull, Darlington, Northumberland, Newcastle, County Durham and Jarrow, in the north-east, whilst others came from the expanding industrial cities of Sheffield, Leeds, and Manchester. Stanley Tock, a labourer at the Hull Flour Mill, enlisted in the 6th East Yorks in August 1914. He was one of eight brothers who would be serving in the Army and Navy by 1915. During the Gallipoli Campaign, four of the Tock brothers were serving in the Dardanelles; two brothers were in the Royal Navy, one a gun layer, whilst Wilfred Wilson Tock was serving in the RAMC and Stanley in the East Yorkshire Regiment.

It was to the harsh summer sun and unforgiving environment of the Dardanelles that the 6th East Yorks set sail from Avonmouth, onboard the R.M.T Franconia at 8.45pm on the 1st July 1915 with a contingent of 27 Officers, one M.O and 955 other ranks. In command of the battalion was Henry Glanville Allen Moore, the 49 year old son of a Dorset vicar. In 1886 Moore had joined the ranks of the Grenadier Guards and was gazetted 2nd Lieutenant in 1891. He was promoted to captain in 1898, when he served in the Egyptian Campaign. Also onboard the R.M.T Franconia were men from the Wiltshire Regiment and details from the Royal Engineers and the Royal Welsh Fusiliers numbering 2,600 men. Due to the fear of a submarine attack, she was escorted by two destroyers for the first 12 hours of the voyage. The threat of attack, meant that armed sections and platoons were deployed across the ship's several decks, whilst the battalion's two machine guns were mounted aft on C deck. The long seaward journey was punctuated by Reveille, beginning at 6am with daily parades, physical training, marksmanship, boat drill and the inspection of the armed platoons every evening at 6pm. On the 7th July, after sighting the African Coast, the men of the Wiltshire Regiment took over all guard duties onboard allowing the men of the 6th East Yorks time to relax and compete in sports and boxing matches. On the 8th July, the Franconia entered the Grand Harbour at Malta, mooring close to the Hospital Ship Rewa, where she began coaling and taking on water. After taking on 25 Details of Blue Jackets from the Royal Naval Division, the vessel set sail for Alexandria passing the H.M.T Empress waiting to enter the Grand Harbour. Two weeks after leaving English shores the Franconia reached Lemnos, with the battalion disembarking at Mudros Bay, where they bivouacked and set up working parties on the afternoon of the 15th July. The duration of July passed with men being formed into working parties whilst Lieutenant H. W Stubbs and

Stanley Tock, 6th East Yorks, one of 120 wounded 21-22 August

the C.O were taken to hospital with sunburn and cramp. The Battalion War Diary states that all the men were in general good health although almost everyone from the battalion was suffering from severe diarrhoea. On the 3rd August, 500 men from "A" & "B" companies arrived at Imbros and practised embarking and disembarking from lighters to destroyers, whilst the rest of the battalion were being given their second inoculations against cholera. Lieutenant Colonel Henry Glanville Allen Moore had attempted to visit the Australian trenches at Anzac prior to the offensive but was prevented from landing due to rough weather.

An Australian sniping position at Anzac

The landings at Suvla Bay on the 6-7th August were intended to break the four month deadlock on Gallipoli, which had begun after the initial landings of the 25th April. Besides providing reinforcements to the ANZACS, they were to act as a supporting attack, with the 6th East Yorks part of an amphibious landing being made by the 10th and 11th Divisions five miles away. The 11th Division, part of Kitchener's New Armies, were making their first attack of the war in conjunction with others being made by the Australians on the formidable Turkish trenches at Lone Pine and the Nek, whilst the New Zealanders would assault the summit of Chunuk Bair.

The other battalions making up the 32nd Brigade were the Yorkshire Regiment, the West Yorkshire Regiment, the West Riding Regiment and the York and Lancaster Regiment. They were part of over 20,000 British troops required to take a relatively low lying range of hills several miles inland. The Suvla Bay area was known to be sparsely defended and it was hoped that the East Yorkshiremen would be able to make a surprise attack, capturing the surrounding hills before Turkish reinforcements could be brought up. The exotic names of the locations the 10th and 11th Divisions were expected to secure and hold were Lala Baba, Chocolate Hill, Tekke Tepe and Suvla Point whilst the great dried up salt lake was a prominent geographical feature. With very limited opposition expected, (around 1,500 Turkish troops and a range of hills between two to five miles inland), it was hoped that the fresh troops would be able to secure and achieve their objectives. But as with so much of the Dardanelles Campaign, a mixture of logistical confusion and poor intelligence which could easily have been acquired before hand was desperately lacking. If the men of the 11th Division were totally in the dark as to their objectives, with many actually believing they were going to Egypt, their officers were little more enlightened. With very few of them having seen a map of the area that they were expected to lead hundreds of men across and hold. Secrecy at GHQ level had prevailed leaving the night landings at unknown locations dangerously lacking in geographical knowledge and ensuring that some battalions were landed on the wrong beaches often in view of the watching Turks. It is important to consider the conditions that the men were facing during the August attacks at Suvla and Anzac in what was the hottest month of the campaign when temperatures regularly reached over 110 degrees Fahrenheit.

At around 8.50 pm on the 6th August, 775 officers and men of the 6th East Yorks left Imbros for Suvla Bay onboard HMS Thesus, whilst 3 officers and 153 other ranks were left in reserve at Imbros. Whilst being regarded as fresh fit troops by Sir Ian Hamilton, they had yet to be tested in battle. Many men would have been dehydrated, weakened by diarrhoea and dysentery, whilst suffering from sunburn and reactions to their recent cholera injections. The supply of fresh drinking water was a continuous problem throughout the campaign, whilst the men went forward on the night of the 6th with no kit but carrying haversacks full of ammunition. The Battalion Diary states that the landing at the horseshoe-shaped Suvla Bay was unopposed but for a few stray shots, with the men coming ashore in boisterous spirits before setting foot on soft sand on C Beach sometime after 11.00 pm. By this time and during the early hours the 32nd Brigade were involved in the fight for the first of their objectives, with the hill of La Baba being finally taken in the early hours of the 7th. As dawn broke, Turkish artillery targeted the newly occupied trenches causing 12 casualties. After their first action of the war, the battalion remained in reserve during the 7th with the men witnessing for the first time the affects of the Turkish guns on the attacking battalions of the 32nd Brigade. Orders were received on the 8th for the East Yorkshire men to attack alongside the 9th West Yorkshire Regiment and secure and hold a section between Chocolate Hill and Sulajik. The short, thorny scrub that covered much of the interior of the peninsula proved fatal for many men enabling the Turks to make good use of its cover for sniping. Captain Rogers was shot and killed by snipers concealed in the scrub, whilst several men were fired upon as they went to draw water from a well. Like so many of the actions that took place across Gallipoli, many tragic defeats could have been resounding victories but through a mixture of indecisiveness, lack of clear orders and objectives, combined with a poor knowledge of the terrain, they became wasted opportunities resulting in the usual heavy loss of life. The Official Historian of the East Yorkshire Regiment, Everard Wyrall, writing just over a decade later, states just how critical time was. "The 8th August 1915 at Suvla held many opportunities for victory or defeat when the fate of Turkey and Constantinople rested on the strategist German General Liman von Sanders". Three separate officer led patrols were sent out throughout Sunday 8th to ascertain the strength of the opposition but as darkness fell no evidence of the Turkish reinforcements was evident, meaning that either they had not been spotted, or more likely they arrived during the early hours. Two Turkish divisions were force-marched across the peninsula ensuring that the weakened defenders position changed dramatically. The key position of Tekke Tepe became lost to the arriving Turkish divisions, but not before around 100 men from "D" Company 6th East Yorkshire Regiment would attempt to reach the summit.

Late and imprecise orders were sent for withdrawal from Scimitar Hill on the early evening of the 8th, but it was not until much later in the evening that these orders were actually received by the scattered battalions of the 32nd Brigade. Time would prove to be critical in the coming action. In the early hours of Monday 9th August at around 03.30, the order to attack Tekke Tepe was received. The Battalion War Diary records a sense of confusion and lack of direction.

> *"After some confusion exhausted men went into trenches during the dark whilst orders were received at 03.30 somewhat late to attack Tekke Tepe (119.0.2) at dawn whilst the West Riding Regiment would attack Kavala Tepe.*

The physical condition of the men during the early hours of the 9th was one of extreme exhaustion and hunger, with the men having eaten little more than bully beef and biscuits for breakfast the previous day. The four companies moved off as dawn was breaking and typical of many Battalion Commanders, Colonel Moore, a physically fit man, was at the head of "D" Company leading the advance. The companies of the 6th East Yorks would later become separated, isolated and unsure of how to proceed across the hilly terrain. The Battalion Diary quite clearly states that Lieutenant Colonel Moore had given verbal orders that "D" and "B" Companies should form the first line of attack, with "D" Company on the left and "B" on the right but this would not happen after they became separated. Due to sheer exhaustion, the three companies were some distance behind "D" Company, who had begun to advance up the lower slopes of the hill without waiting for support and with an absence of explicit instructions. Little opposition had initially been encountered but they were beginning to be picked off by Turkish snipers from concealed trenches and positions as they climbed the hill. There can be little doubt that due to Colonel Moore's determination to reach and secure the summit of Tekke Tepe by way of a rapid ascent of the hill without waiting for "B"Company, the men of "D" company were left ineffective and vulnerable when they encountered much larger Turkish forces. It is unclear just how far Moore and the survivors of his party climbed up the hill, for the 9th was a day of confused, unrecorded action and dispatches were lost. The action of the three companies at the slope of Tekke Tepe and the farm at Sulajik have been for the most part, omitted from the Battalion Diary in favour of that of "D" Company's ascent up the hill. The Historian of the East Yorkshire Regiment, Everard Wyrall, states that Lieutenant Colonel Moore, Captain Elliot, and Lieutenants Rawstone and J.Still reached the summit, whilst some historians tend to take the view that their party did not get that far, with a deep fold blocking their ascent. Whatever their final position on the hill, with too few men it could only have been a brief symbolic gesture. With the three companies still at the base of the hill the outcome was inevitable, although a sergeant major and several men did manage to escape the enveloping Turks descending en masse down Tekke Tepe. Initially, the small group, which numbered four officers and up to 20 men, were posted as missing. Heavily outnumbered, Lieutenant Colonel Henry Glanville Allen Moore, who would later be mentioned in dispatches, saw that their position was hopeless and, against sacrificing the lives of his men for no possible gain ordered his men to lay down their arms. Weak and exhausted, the 49 year old father of two daughters was knelt by a ravine with his back turned when an unseen Turkish soldier bayoneted him through the back, in what was a cowardly and unnecessary act of murder on a defenseless man who had just surrendered. The surviving officers, Captain R.D Elliot, and Lieutenant R.A Rawstone and 2nd Lieutenant J Still, were taken before German General Liman Von Sanders. The three officers and around 12 men were just some of those posted as missing,

Lieutenant Colonel. Henry Glanville Allen Moore Commanding 6th East Yorks

whilst Moore's death was officially accepted on the 11th August, making him the third Battalion Commander of the East Yorkshire Regiment killed since the outbreak of the war.

Fighting and advancing up the lower slopes without artillery support, the remaining platoons of the 6th East Yorks were eventually forced to retreat after losing two machine guns. They managed to form a firing line with men from the West Riding Regiment. After being outflanked, they were forced to retire, with men coming under fire from many unseen Turks on all sides. Moore's heroic but somewhat reckless advance earlier that morning, without knowing the strength of the enemy and going forward without "B" Company, was the first of a series of uncoordinated actions, which eventually resulted in lost ground and very heavy losses. The Battalion War Diary discreetly apportions a degree of blame to Moore for his rapid ascent of Tekke Tepe. This left "A" "B" and "C" Companies well to the rear with unclear orders whilst Major E Bray's own diary account shows his frustration and anger at the reserves, who failed to move forward in support later in the day when they fought for around three hours around the farm at Sulajik that afternoon. The many missing men meant that the casualties for the action of the 9th August were not fully known for several weeks. Some men were taken prisoner but the majority of those listed as missing had been killed and the number of dead rose considerably from that recorded in the Battalion War Diary. Lieutenant Colonel Moore was one of those posted as missing, with his death confirmed on the 11th August. After the action of the 8-9th, the 775 officers and other ranks that had landed on the evening of the 6th had suffered over 335 casualties, amounting to 44 per cent of the attacking battalion whilst 15 of 24 officers had been killed, wounded, or were missing.

Killed	Wounded	Wounded & Missing	Missing	Total
20	104	28	183	335

The sheer nature of an offensive or a chaotic retreat similar to the one which the 6th East Yorks were involved in means that anything approaching accurate casualty figures could not be known for many weeks afterwards. Only the deaths of those men witnessed by surviving comrades were listed as killed in the casualty lists. Many others whose whereabouts were unknown were posted as missing, giving relatives a glimmer of hope that their loved ones may have been taken prisoner or were lying wounded in a hospital. The casualty figures of the 9th August bore out the chaotic and desperate nature of the engagement, with just 6 per cent of the battalion's casualties being confirmed as killed, whilst over 200 men were posted as missing. With the fate of so many men unknown, relatives clung to hope, whilst others actively advertised through the local newspapers the Hull Daily Mail and Hull Daily News, for any news of their husbands and sons.

Two months after the action of 9th August, the desperate mother of 24 year old

Pte. William Fewlass Atkinson, Missing

Sgt. Thomas Wing, Missing

William Fewlass Atkinson, who was still officially listed as missing, placed a heartfelt plea in the Hull Daily Mail asking for information from anyone who had served with her son or that may have been with him in hospital. Like so many other Hull men, his death would be officially recorded as 9th August 1915.

Thomas Wing, from Lime Tree Avenue, Garden Village, was another local man posted missing on the 9th. A former Territorial, he enlisted in the 6th East Yorks in August 1914. Due to his military experience and knowledge he was soon promoted to sergeant. Like many other men, he was initially posted as missing, until his death was officially recorded as Monday 9th August.

Pte. Herbert Ernest Thompson, "D" Company, Missing 9 August

Herbert Ernest Thompson, a 31 year old Hull Dock Labourer serving with "D" Company, had been one of those attacking uphill with Lieutenant Colonel Moore. Similar to over 200 men from the battalion he was also posted as missing on the 9th. Living on Strickland Street, Hessle Road, his mother was one of several local women appealing for news of her son weeks later through the Hull Daily Mail. Tragically, she had lost her only other son serving with the

1/4th East Yorks just two months earlier, whilst Herbert's death was later officially confirmed as the 9th August 1915.

Besides the many East Yorkshire men amongst the ranks of the 6th East Yorks at Gallipoli, other local men were serving with numerous different regiments at the Dardanelles. Lieutenant G Wooll, a Beverley man who had risen through the ranks, was killed with the Northumberland Fusiliers. The 6th Service Battalion the Lincolnshire Regiment, like the 6th East Yorks, were part of Kitchener's New Armies and were involved in the attack on Hill 70 (Scimitar Hill) on Monday 9th August. Like "Black Week" during the Boer War, Monday 9th at Suvla became known as "Black Monday," with the 6th Lincolnshire Regiment suffering horrendous casualties of 12 of it's 17 officers and 390 other ranks killed, wounded and missing from the 561 that set out. The desperate fight for survival that day amidst so much chaos left men being subjected to intense Turkish artillery fire, which resulted in the dry scrub and bush catching fire, burning wounded men alive. With thick black smoke and much of the ground on fire, many men were prevented from retreating and they were now coming under fire from British artillery. The 9th of August can only be described as a total disaster and one of great loss Constantinople had been saved from the guns of the Royal Navy whilst the Turks celebrated but the Allies chance had gone. "Black Monday" left many hundreds of men unaccounted for, officially listed as missing. In addition to the large death toll, up to 10,000 men were evacuated during the coming days. Unlike many Battalion War Diaries which generally just list officer casualties the 6th East Yorks is very detailed, listing many of the injured and those later returning to active service.

The battalion received its first reinforcements on Friday 13th August, with three officers and 153 NCOs and men arriving from Imbros. In the following days, the remnants of the battalion assumed their official role as the Division's Pioneer battalion under the command of Major, Malcolm Gordon Cowper. Their task of entrenching across the low ground south-east of Lala Baba was explained to them by Lieutenant Colonel Bland of the Royal Engineers. Turkish artillery on the peninsula had caused heavy casualties but the number and quality of guns was not comparable to those in France and Flanders, whilst for the allies the limited ground they held restricted the movement of their artillery. It was the close proximity of the men to the enemy that ensured troops were never truly safe. A Turkish shell fell on a platoon of the 6th East Yorks when out of the line and in the process of bivouacking, killing one man and wounding six. With their backs to the sea and every foot of ground at a premium the cramped conditions are recorded in the Battalion War Diary, with "A" and "C" Companies having no beach at all and having to dig themselves into the sides of the cliffs. Similar orders had been issued earlier when Sir Ian Hamilton had given complex instructions to new battalions to "dig dig dig until you are safe". Fatigue parties numbering between 100-200 men set off under cover of darkness, commencing work at 20.00 and carrying on until dawn. Under the supervision of a R.E officer, the communication trenches around Chocolate Hill were deepened and strengthened.

The Battle of Scimitar Hill, 21-22 August 1915

The intended capture of Scimitar Hill and 'W' Hill, launched in conjunction with the attack on Hill 60, would be the last major offensive of the campaign. Intended to link Anzac Cove and Suvla Bay, some four miles apart, it was essential to capture Hill 60, the singular prominent feature between the two locations. It would also be the last time during the campaign that the 6th East Yorks, a pioneer battalion, would be asked to fight as infantry on the peninsula. Similar to the Germans on the Western Front, the Turks held much of the high ground and with their backs to the sea and crammed into narrow bridgeheads around the cliffs and the landing beaches, the British were constantly being forced to breakout from their tight confines. The objectives of the 9th had proved to be unachievable but it was hoped that this offensive involving the 11th and 29th Divisions would be able to strengthen the exposed Suvla Bay landing beaches. The East Yorkshire men along with other battalions from the 11th Division were to attack "W" Hill.

On Thursday 19th August, after being in reserve since the 9th, the fatigue parties working on the cliff dug outs and mule lines listened to the distant noise of shell and rifle fire. The following day at dusk, the battalion was ordered to relieve the Northumberland Fusiliers in the trenches south-east of Chocolate Hill. Reserve trenches were dug under cover of darkness, with the battalion being attached to the 34th Brigade 11th Division. It was ordered to support the Dorsets and Lancashire Fusiliers who were then occupying the fire trench 400 metres to their front. The mid-afternoon attack was to begin after a 30 minute artillery bombardment. Almost as if an organised natural conspiracy was put into operation, low cloud and haze hampered the joint bombardment by the Royal Navy and artillery, obscuring many of the earlier targets singled out. The beginning of the bombardment alerted the Turks that an attack was imminent, ensuring that they were able to respond with rifle and artillery fire into the advancing battalions. The joint bombardment began at 14.30 precisely and lasted until 15.00, when the Dorsets and Lancashire Fusiliers went forward in two lines towards the enemy trenches at Hetman Chair and Aire Kavak. A platoon of the 6th East Yorks would occupy and hold the recently vacated trenches to their front, whilst the rest of the battalion would support the two advancing battalions. The Dorsets and Lancashire Fusiliers stormed into the first Turkish trench, putting several Turks to the bayonet before they broke and ran, leaving the East Yorks to cover over 300 metres of ground before they reached the trenches previously held by the two attacking battalions. The Battalion Diary describes the heavy artillery and rifle fire the men came under at 15.00 hours.

> *"Throughout the entire advance we came under a storm of heavy rifle and shell fire. We could not move beyond the first Turkish trench which was some 300-400 metres in front of the fire trench. The battalion was now spread along 300 metres of the abandoned Turkish trench with men of the Dorsets and Lancashire Fusiliers intermingled amongst our ranks. Some 100 men occupied the Azmak Dere ravine where an advance was made towards the orchard but with very heavy casualties sustained the order to retire was given. Orders were then given to entrench along the ravine with a barricade of sandbags erected across the ravine and up to the end of the trench. Several Turkish counter attacks were made during the night but these were not pushed home, whilst many of our officers were killed during this time.*

One of the officers killed during this period was Lieutenant George Hamilton Mee, a 32 year old Hertfordshire man. He was shot through the heart and killed instantly whilst leading men forward in an attempt to outflank the probing Turkish attacks around the Azmak Dere. Just two platoons from 7th Battalion South Staffordshire Regiment, numbering around 100 men, were received as reinforcements but these men were all immediately employed in holding the firing line in the ravine. There were several further requests throughout the night for reinforcements, stretchers to evacuate the many wounded and ammunition, only the latter was supplied. Whilst messages came back saying that support was on its way, the Battalion War Diary clearly states that none materialized. Despite the lack of support and aid for the wounded, ammunition was plentifully supplied, with small parties of men bringing it up to the ravine and the barricades where it was passed down the line hand by hand along the captured Turkish trench. The fighting continued throughout the night and into the early hours of the morning, with the casualties of Hull men registered on both the 21-22nd August. The proximity of the trenches on the peninsula meant that bombs were an effective weapon which could be easily thrown into the enemy trenches. Many improvised bombs were made from jam jars when their reserve ran out. Under the cover of darkness, a group of Turkish bombers crawled through the long grass, getting within 30 metres of the barricade. They were able to launch large numbers of cricket ball bombs at the trench and over the defences, although many of them fell short. By 05.00 hours on the 22nd, the much reduced 6th battalion were struggling to hold out and were forced to retire. Major, Malcolm Gordon Cowper, who had taken over command after the death of the C.O on the 9th, arrived at a critical moment. He immediately asserted his authority, ordering the men to stand fast and form a new firing line. Major Cowper was later wounded and taken to the rear and during the next two hours the battalion fell back to their original trenches 300 metres to the rear, fighting as they went whilst coming under heavy rifle and shrapnel fire.

Hull casualties August 21-22

On the morning of the 21st August, the 6th East Yorks numbered 512 officers and men and would suffer casualties of 40 per cent, with Stanley Tock one of over 120 men wounded. James Adams, Richard Airy, John Andrews, James F. Banks, Ernest Boyes, Charles Dearing, John Emery, Charles Everatt, Richard Harrison, Frederick Joyce, Walter Morrod, John Walker and John E. Wood were all Hull men killed during the 21-22nd August. The casualty lists below were recorded on the evening of the 22nd after roll call and would have risen during the coming days, with Henry H Nicholson, from Holderness Road in Hull, being one of those after he died of wounds on 28th. One in four casualties were posted as missing, whilst 5 out of 12 officers had been killed, none of them Hull men.

Killed	Wounded	Missing	Total
22	128	49	199

In less than two weeks, the 6th East Yorkshire Pioneer Battalion had been involved in two desperate and disastrous actions. These, like so many others, had promised so much but had resulted in failure, costing the battalion over 500 casualties, with around 50 Hull men losing their lives on 9th. Never again did the 6th East Yorks fight as infantrymen on the peninsula and the battalion became engaged in what it had been trained for during the next four months. Despite being out of the line, as trench warfare stagnated, men were still being evacuated to hospital on Lemnos in significant numbers. The detailed War Diary shows that around 38 men were sent to hospital, many for sickness, in October whilst 23 returned to the battalion. The Greek Island of Lemnos was some 65 miles from the peninsula. It was there that the wounded and sick men were evacuated to. The natural deep-water harbour at Mudros, was an essential supply depot and hospital base, just a few hours sailing time from Gallipoli. Hundreds of vessels of various size and class, including hospital ships, trawlers, and warships, could be berthed or anchored off Mudros Harbour. After a brief spell at Mudros, the battalion sailed for Imbros, where they spent all of January, until embarking to work on the Suez Canal in February 1916.

Casualty figures for the eight-month campaign can vary significantly. Conservative figures record the deaths of over 56,000 Allied soldiers killed in action or dying from wounds, including 10,000 Frenchmen. Estimated Turkish deaths range from 57,000-80,000. What is certain is that at least 100,000 men lost their lives on a narrow strip of land just 40 miles in length and 12 miles wide. For the young nations of Australia and New Zealand with their fledgling populations, the losses were devastating. Around 8,000 Australians and 2,600 New Zealanders were killed, whilst 1,300 Indian troops died.

Failure and Evacuation, December 1915

Much of the failure for the Suvla Bay landings is laid squarely on the shoulders of Victorian Generals. Australian Military Historian, John Laffin, viewed Lieutenant General, Sir Frederick Stopford as the most incompetent of all the Corps Commanders foisted on Sir Ian Hamilton from London. With many of the most able and experienced Generals engaged on the Western Front, 61 year old Lieutenant General Frederick Stopford was a career soldier, with experience in the wars of Empire. However, his strengths were limited to staff work and ceremonial duties. Plucked from his obscure post as the Lieutenant of the Tower of London, his appointment at Suvla Bay was vastly beyond his experience and military capabilities. His woefully ineffective leadership which culminated in the disastrous August offensive at Suvla, meant that he was relieved of his command and sent back to England in disgrace.

Lieutenant General, Sir Frederick Stopford

Although somewhat disrespectful to the British Army, who were suffering equally to the ANZACS, Peter Weir's 1981 film, "Gallipoli" starring a young Mel Gibson in the leading role would sum up the tragedy of the campaign and the incompetence of many of the Generals. There were certainly grave mistakes made by the British High Command and again, lack of intelligence would result in the close, intense slaughter of hundreds of troopers from the Australian Light Horse. In fifteen minutes, four separate waves numbering over 450 men were shot down whilst attacking the formidable Turkish positions at the Nek, leaving over 230 of them dead in one of the most concentrated killing zones of the war.

Ironically for many combatants and historians the only successful operation of the eight month campaign were the evacuations, which were carried out in December and in early January at Anzac and Suvla, without loss. A series of improvised disguises, which included water cans triggered to fire rifles and explosions, were constructed to cover the evacuation. Down from remote hills and trenches, some less than 10 yards from the Turkish positions, trudged groups of men wearing sacking around their boots to deaden the noise, whilst strict orders ensured the withdrawal was carried out in total silence. The logistics of evacuating more than 130,000 men and thousands of animals in December was immense, with ships and barges only able to approach the beaches and coves under cover of darkness. The French also began to evacuate their troops in December and if the Turks were aware of the withdrawal then they did little to disrupt it. By January 1916, the last troops were taken off the peninsula, in a remarkable feat of stealth and deception as great as any in the war.

Chapter 6 — Hull Men at the Front in 1914-15

Mule Gully, Anzac Cove

The Suez Canal circa 1914

Evacuation Order from Gallipoli, Thursday 17th December 1915

The strict evacuation orders from the peninsula were issued by Lieutenant Colonel, Cecil Loraine Estridge, commanding the 6th Service Battalion East Yorkshire Regiment in November 1915.

Just four months after their arrival, the survivors of the 6th East Yorks slipped away to Imbros and then to Egypt in February 1916, whilst other East Yorkshire men from Kitchener's New Armies, the Hull 92nd Brigade, had arrived in December 1915 to defend the Suez Canal from an anticipated Turkish attack. The war against the Turks, trained and supported by the German Army, would go on in Egypt and Palestine.

1. **Parade** – in full marching order ready to pass starting point 29th Division Rest Camp at 18.45

2. **Orders** – H.Q Signals, Machine Guns, Quarter Master 'C' Company.

3. **Move** – to Field Ambulance path and 29th Division H.Q to point X.

4. **Battalion** – will form en masse on the right facing West Point and stand easy.

5. **Formation** – up at point X numbers will be checked and Orderly Sergeants will report to R.S.M.

6. **Dress** – Greatcoats are to be worn. Complete silence will be observed and no smoking or lights of any kind. There will an officer at the rear of each Company whilst ranks to keep closed up. Several officers will move up and down to prevent noise and maintain discipline. The Battalion will keep to the right of the road and an officer to go in the front of the boat if embarking on lighters. First men will go down below and others will follow them until the lighter is full. Men can unfasten belts and shoulder straps but are not to take off equipment until ordered to. Iron rations which consisted of cheese, tea, biscuits, and one tin of bully beef for every six men will not be touched until orders by the C.O. If the battalion is shelled at X point they will take cover in the evacuated trenches of the Manchesters.

To the Bitter End! December 1915

Only the 1st Battalion from the East Yorkshire Regiment saw active service during 1914, suffering hundreds of casualties at the Aisne and Armentières. But with heavy casualties amongst the BEF it fell to returning garrison troops, Colonials, Territorials, and finally to Kitchener's New Armies, to carry on the war on the Western Front and the new front at the Dardanelles. Part of Kitchener's New Armies, the 6th, 7th and 8th East Yorks had all been raised at Beverley in August and September 1914. A six month syllabus of infantry training had been established for the new armies but with so few available officers and NCO's, adequate programmes were often delayed. This meant that many of the new battalions were not up to the required level six months after their formation, when they had initially been expected to be ready for frontline service. The 6th East Yorks, like many of the New Armies, would not see overseas service until almost a year after their formation. The 2nd East Yorks were the next from the Regiment to arrive at the front in January 1915, followed by 4th East Yorks, a Territorial battalion in April with both battalions being called upon to perform a crucial role during the Second Battle of Ypres. The 2nd East Yorks suffered over 1,030 casualties in just four months, whilst the Hull Territorials and later the 6th East Yorks would each lose hundreds of men in the spring and summer of 1915. By September 1915 the East Yorkshire Regiment had five battalions in France and Flanders whilst the 6th East Yorks were at Gallipoli. The 1st East Yorks had been at the front for exactly a year, whilst even those days recorded as quiet in the Battalion War Diary were resulting in two men killed and five wounded. A year into the war, the trenches had improved significantly. They were deeper, with duckboards to walk upon and had more dugouts, better defences and thicker wire, with a comprehensive network of communication and support trenches. Lieutenant Colonel, John Louis Justin Clarke, 1st Battalion East Yorkshire Regiment, was commanding a battalion of 30 officers and 998 other ranks in autumn 1915.

Lieutenant John Horrocks buried at Poperinghe New Military Cemetery

On Saturday 23rd October 1915 Lieutenant, The Honourable John Horrocks, was found dead in his dugout. His death was recorded as heart failure.

He was the very last of the original 27 officers from the summer of 1914 still serving with the 1st Battalion East Yorkshire Regiment. The death of this able officer, who was also the Battalion Quarter-Master, was noted with sadness in the Regimental War Diary. The war had claimed another victim, if not in the usual way by bullet or shell.

With the new inexperienced battalions coming to the front, the experienced men of the 1st East Yorks were transferred to the 64th Brigade 21st Division to help bring some sense of stability to the new brigades coming into the line. The Service Battalions of the 7th and 8th East Yorkshire Regiment were both in France by September, whilst the 2nd East Yorks left for Salonika in October after suffering 1,360 casualties, 267 of them killed in just nine months, many of them Hull men. As 1915 closed, there were ten Battalions of the East Yorkshire Regiment in action overseas. Four were in France, one, the 2nd Battalion, had left for Greece whilst the 92nd Brigade, made up entirely of the four Hull Pals Battalions had left for Egypt to join the 6th Battalion fresh from Gallipoli. It had taken over a year for the new Service Battalions to be ready to serve at the front but by the end of 1915, they were at the front in their thousands, with the 92nd Brigade finally reaching the Western Front 18 months after their formation. As 1916 began, the deadlock showed no sign of breaking with the Germans attacking the French at Verdun and the slaughter increasing to a new ferocity. Hull casualties of 1916 were more than double those of 1915, whilst the war would have to be endured for a further three years.

Chapter Seven

You're needed now! Conscription Looms

Hull Telephone Company staff enlist at the Hull City Hall December 1915

In 1914, the raising of Kitchener's New Armies had been hugely successful, with some 1,186,335 men having volunteered by the end of the year. That included the formation of 404 Service Battalions, making up the New Armies. But as 1915 opened, those enlisting began to drop to around 100,000 a month, with just 71,600 men enlisting in September 1915. Unlike her European counterparts, where military service had long been compulsory, Britain had never compelled men to serve in the army and not since the press gangs of the Napoleonic wars had men been actively forced into military service. Prime Minister Herbert Asquith's liberal principles meant that he was still against conscription a year into the war but with a reshaped cabinet from May 1915, the cross party coalition, which was made up of 40 per cent of Tory ministers, was becoming split on compulsory military service. Lloyd George went against the liberal stance of voluntary recruitment whilst several Tories were against their party line, which was one of compulsory military service. The "shell scandal" of May had highlighted that the munitions

SHORT SERVICE.
(For the Duration of the War, with the Colours and in the Army Reserve).

ATTESTATION OF

No. 228137. Name Geo. Dinsdale Corps R.E. I.W.T.

Card No. 13 / 32

Questions to be put to the Recruit before Enlistment.

1. What is your Name? — George Dinsdale
2. What is your full Address? — 1 Wallis Place, Nottingale, Hull
3. Are you a British Subject? — Yes
4. What is your Age? — 21 Years 3 Months
5. What is your Trade or Calling? — Boatman
6. Are you Married? — Yes
7. Have you ever served in any branch of His Majesty's Forces, naval or military, if so, which? — No
8. Are you willing to be vaccinated or re-vaccinated? — Yes
9. Are you willing to be enlisted for General Service? — Yes
10. Did you receive a Notice, and do you understand its meaning, and who gave it to you? — Yes. Name: Sergt. Purdue
11. Are you willing to serve upon the following conditions... — Yes

Religion: C of E

I, George Dinsdale, do solemnly declare that the above answers made by me to the above questions are true, and that I am willing to fulfil the engagements made.

George Dinsdale — SIGNATURE OF RECRUIT
Arthur Souter — Signature of Witness

OATH TO BE TAKEN BY RECRUIT ON ATTESTATION.

I, George Dinsdale, swear by Almighty God, that I will be faithful and bear true Allegiance to His Majesty King George the Fifth, His Heirs, and Successors, and that I will, as in duty bound, honestly and faithfully defend His Majesty, His Heirs, and Successors, in Person, Crown, and Dignity against all enemies, and will observe and obey all orders of His Majesty, His Heirs and Successors, and of the Generals and Officers set over me. So help me God.

CERTIFICATE OF MAGISTRATE OR ATTESTING OFFICER.

The Recruit above named was cautioned by me that if he made any false answer to any of the above questions he would be liable to be punished as provided in the Army Act.

The above questions were then read to the Recruit in my presence.

I have taken care that he understands each question, and that his answer to each question has been duly entered as replied to, and the said Recruit has made and signed the declaration and taken the oath before me at CENTRAL HULL RECRT. on this _____ day of 8 DEC 1915 19.

Signature of the Justice H.H. Watt

† Certificate of Approving Officer.

I certify that this Attestation of the above-named Recruit is correct, and properly filled up, and that the required... If enlisted by special authority, Army Form B. 203 (or other authority for the enlistment)...

30 JAN 1917

Place Sandwich

CAPTAIN, R.E. INLAND WATER TRANSPORT — Approving Officer

industry was of equal importance, whilst the numbers of those enlisting meant the needs of industry had to be balanced, ensuring key essential workers were not lost to the army, as had been the case in 1914. The National Registration Act of August 1915 was intended to allow the government to evaluate just how many men it had for the War effort after essential workers were deducted. All those aged between 15 and 65 were required to register whilst men employed on the railway, in the coal mines, and in agriculture were given exemption stars. The result of this survey highlighted the fact that there were over 5 million men of military age, some 12 per cent of the population, who had not enlisted, with over 1.5 million single men who were not in starred occupations and were immediately eligible for military service. As the war deepened, the age limit was increased, whilst the required physical attributes of those needed was reduced.

Locally, it was estimated that some 19,727 Hull men had enlisted by March 1915, some 27 per cent of the local men who would go on to serve during the course of the war. National Registration took place in Hull on 15th August 1915, with the names and occupations of all men of military age being compiled and handed to the Recruiting Authorities. At the City Hall, over 500 voluntary clerks were engaged in the labourious task of compiling the register of Hull men eligible for service. But their temporary status meant that a more permanent staff was required and Major Douglas Boyd successfully secured the services of 100 female teachers, who were accommodated at the Hull City Hall to complete the task. Nationally, Asquith's reluctance to impose compulsory service ensured a final compromise was reached, with Lord Derby's scheme being implemented in October, in an attempt to supplement the required shortfall of those who had been voluntarily enlisting.

November 30th 1915 was initially the closing date for voluntary Attestation but due to a late surge this was extended into the middle of December. Across Hull, there was a clamour to attest in the autumn of 1915. Entire workforces from Thomas Wilson Sons & Co, the Hull Telephone Company, and the 12 staff from the Sculcoates Workhouse on Beverley Road, (which included the labour master) being just some of those companies enlisting in November and December.

The Prime Minister's personal pledge to married men in November 1915 stated that they would only be called up after all the single men and widowers with no dependent children had gone before. Bachelors were listed separately to married men, although men who married after that time were not included, whilst the youngest married men would only be summoned after all the various groups of single men had been called up. Because men had attested for military service it did not mean that they would necessarily be called up immediately. This was dependent on several factors, their marital status, age and particular profession. Men in occupations regarded as essential to the war effort received stars, whilst appeals made through their employers could be made against their attestation. George Dinsdale, a married man employed as a Dock Pilot and Boatman, was not called up until January 1917. This was 13 months after he had attested. He was later placed in a unit with the Royal Engineers, the Inland Water Transport Section, where his maritime knowledge could be put to best use by the military. With thousands of Hull men attesting for service through the Derby Scheme, some 12,000 were processed at the City Hall in just three days, (although nationally it did not achieve the numbers required from across the rest of the country). After being reassured by Asquith that they would be called up last, it was married men who made up the greater numbers of those attesting whilst just over one million single men, (half of the available number) came forward. This ensured that the voluntary system had failed to attract the numbers of men required for the war effort.

During the early months of the war, Hull established its own Recruiting Committee, with Sir Erik Ohlson presiding over the work carried out from Hull City Hall. But after the Military Service Act of 1916, recruitment was taken over by the Ministry of National Service. With Conscription came the right to appeal against military service through some 1,800 Local Tribunals which were operating across the country. The introduction of the Military Service Act became law in January 1916, meaning single men aged 18-41 were immediately eligible for military service unless employed in a reserved profession. The parameters of those eligible for military service changed during the war, with the age limit being increased upwards as the war continued. With the increasingly hostile reaction to men not wearing uniform, it was realised that essential workers employed in the war effort had to have something visible to signify their status to the general public. Silver badges and armbands were issued to workers in reserved occupations, whilst soldiers home on long term sick leave were issued with blue uniforms and silver wound badges to save them from abuse and the dreaded white feather.

Although over 2,400,000 men had volunteered by December 1915 this was not enough. Asquith's hope that men could be persuaded to enlist voluntarily in sufficient numbers had failed and it was realised by 17th December 1915 that men would have to be compelled to serve in one branch of the military by an Act of Parliament. The Military Service Act received Royal Assent in January 1916 and became law. Despite the Prime Minister's pledge, young married men were being called up just two months later and by May total conscription meant that both single and married men aged 18-41 were eligible to be called up.

Chapter Eight

What Became of the Men of 1914-15?

In 1914 it was left to a young but professional British Army, combined with thousands of older veterans of Empire who were called back to service during the nation's hour of need. Better trained and equipped than any British Army before them, their ranks would be decimated by December 1914. In 1915 it would be left to the Territorials, Colonials and men of Kitcheners New Armies to carry on the fight.

The following pages contain the stories of just a few of the men at war in 1914-15. Those who survived the war often led very different lives. Although all were affected by the war, some more profoundly than others, many came home and buried their memories, raised families and went back to work for local companies. In the words of the German Author Erich Maria Remarque "Whilst the survivors may have escaped its shells many of them were destroyed by war". Some lived relatively short lives, dying before the end of the Second World War, whilst others lived well into old age.

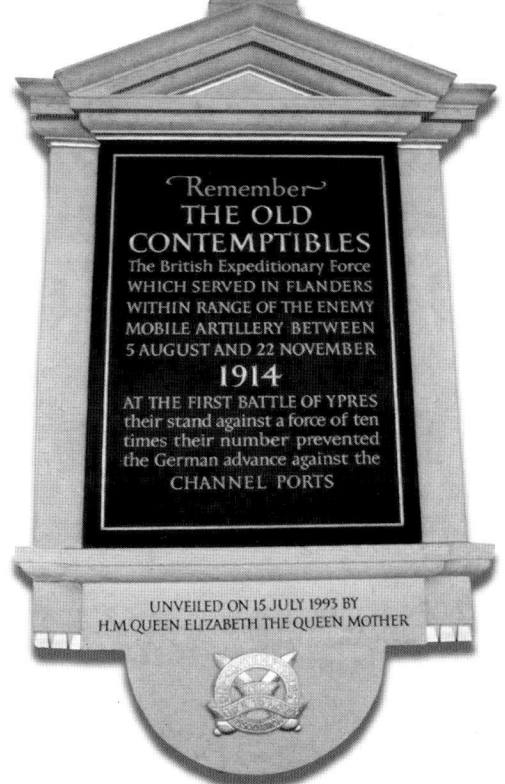

2nd Lieutenant Merton Beckwith-Smith
1st Battalion Coldstream Guards

Born in Sussex, Old Etonian, Merton Beckwith-Smith, was an archetypical officer of the time and would have been in command of several of the Hull Coldstreamers in 1914. Aged 24, 2nd Lieutenant Merton Beckwith-Smith led one of the first bayonet charges of the war, which was an early trench raid. He was so nearly killed after his platoon was ordered to take and secure two German trenches in October 1914, with his life being saved by Corporal R. Russell. A month later, after the First Battle of Ypres, the 1st Battalion Coldstream Guards had been reduced to less than 100 men and with casualties amongst junior officers so high his survival throughout the duration of the war was remarkable. Merton Beckwith-Smith finished the war as a major and spent the rest of his life in the army. His death would take place some 28 years later during the Second World War; then a 52 year old major-general. He was taken prisoner by the Japanese after the fall of Singapore and died in 1942 in a prisoner of war camp thousands of miles away from the battlefields of Flanders that he had known in his youth.

Pte. 10348 Frederick Livingston Thorrold
2nd Battalion Coldstream Guards

Almost one in three of the Hull men serving with the Coldstream Guards that I have researched had been killed by the end of 1914, whilst one in two had been wounded. Frederick Thorrold, of 56, Dalton Street Hull, had been injured in September when he wrote home to his mother describing his experiences at the Aisne and how much the Germans feared the bayonet. Thorrold was shot twice through the left arm during action at the Aisne. By 1915 he had been transferred to the 4th Reserve Battalion Coldstream Guards, when on 29th April 1915, Thorrold was medically discharged from the army, with his condition to be re-examined in July 1916. His Medical Report states "general good health, but excessive stammering and severe nervous symptoms preventing him from carrying out the duties of a soldier although these were not considered to be due to his military service".

After being medically discharged, Thorrold re-enlisted in the 4th Reserve Yorkshire Regiment in August 1915 and served for a further 16 months in England. Whilst present in the guardroom at Catterick Barracks in December 1916, he suffered from a series of uncontrollable fits over several days and was diagnosed by a RAMC officer as being epileptic. He was permanently discharged from any future military service in April 1917, when he was granted an army pension. Frederick Livingston Thorrold survived the war by 25 years, dying in Hull in 1943, aged 48.

Frederick William Wollaston
Captain of the Hull Trawler Cameo

Frederick William Wollaston, originally from Preston in Lancashire was born in 1858 and had spent most of his adult life working as a fisherman out of Hull. Captain of the Hull Trawler Cameo at the outbreak of the First World War, he was one of the first on the scene after the Wilson line vessel Runo hit a mine in September 1914. He was honoured by a presentation at the City Hall for his important role in the rescue. Wollaston was aged 60 at the end of the war. He survived the war despite the loss of around 670 local trawlers and minesweepers from across the region, whilst some 14,660 British merchant seamen lost their lives, around 1,200 of them being from Hull. Living at 183, Walton Street, Fred Wollaston died in 1936 aged 78.

L/Cpl 3010 Frederick Charles Ware
Coldstream Guards

Frederick Ware enlisted in the 3rd Battalion Coldstream Guards in October 1899 and served for three years before becoming a Reservist in October 1902, when he left to join the Hull Police Force. Frederick Charles Ware had married Alice Gardham in 1912. Their daughter, Ada Helena, was born the following year and was aged one when war was declared. As a Reservist, he was called back to the colours on 5th August 1914. He was one of several Hull policemen serving with the Coldstream Guards in 1914 and was wounded at Soupir during the battle of the Aisne in September 1914. Ware was one of relatively few men who would survive the entire duration of the war and still be serving in 1918, although he did not spend all of the time at the front as he was posted to the Reserve Battalion back in England in 1916-17. Present in the early battles of 1914 he would see the war end at the front with his original battalion in 1918. Aged 40, he was demobbed in January 1919 at Ripon and returned to his wife and daughter, then aged five, at the family home at 2 Devon Street, Cottingham.

L/Cpl 10985 Stanley Tock
6th Battalion East Yorkshire Regiment

Like many hundreds of Hull men in 1914 Stanley Tock was working in one the city's seed and flourmills. His war began at the end of August 1914 when he joined the 6th East Yorkshire Regiment. After leaving Grantham and after some further training at Witley, he had expected to be sent to the Western Front when the battalion began to prepare for overseas service in April 1915. Stanley was one of four Tock brothers who saw service during the Dardanelles campaign. He was one of over a hundred and twenty men wounded from the 6th East Yorks on the 21/ 22nd August 1915, when the battalion fought their last action of the Gallipoli campaign, suffering heavy casualties. Stanley Tock married sweetheart Hilda Baggaley in 1916. After the war he went to work for Reckitts at their Morley Street factory and lived on Garden Village in company housing, where they brought up several children. Shortly after attending his youngest son's wedding, Stanley Tock died from cancer in 1961, aged 68.

The war-time marriage of Stanley Tock, 1916

Captain Cecil Moorhouse Slack M.C
1/4th Battalion East Yorkshire Regiment

The post war marriage of Cecil Moorhouse Slack, 1919

Cecil Moorhouse Slack was born in Australia in 1893 to an English father and an Australian mother. He was the eldest of several children born to William and Winifred Slack. Aged 17, Cecil began work at Reckitts Head Office on Dansom Lane in 1911, where his father was a Director. In August 1914, he volunteered for overseas service with the 4th East Yorkshire Regiment, a Territorial battalion. Within days of their arrival at Boulogne in April 1915, they were ordered into the frontline at the Second Battle of Ypres suffering heavy casualties amongst their officers and men during April and May, many due to shell fire. Although wounded at the Second Battle of Ypres, Cecil Moorhouse Slack later won the Military Cross and served at the front for a further three years before he was taken prisoner in April 1918, when casualties had reduced the battalion to just 120 men and 3 officers.

In September 1919, Cecil Moorhouse Slack married long-time sweetheart and Nurse Dora Willatt in Hull. They were together for 57 years before her death in 1976. He died in Beverley in 1985, 70 years after the Second Battle of Ypres, which had seen Hull's first heavy casualties of the war and the deaths of so many of his fellow officers. His death, aged 92, meant that he was one of the very last survivors of the battalion.

Pte. 5854 George Harry Wyatt V.C
3rd Battalion Coldstream Guards

George Wyatt, standing front left with others Great War V.C. winners of the Guards Brigades

In common with many other men serving with the Guards Brigades in 1914, George Harry Wyatt joined the Barnsley Police Force after leaving the Coldstream Guards in 1908. The son of a veterinary surgeon, he was an accomplished horseman and had served with the police mounted section. At the outbreak of war, he had recently been transferred to the Doncaster Police Force and as a Reservist, he found himself back in the army six years after his service had ended. George Harry Wyatt earned the highest award for gallantry whilst serving with the 3rd Battalion Coldstream Guards, in only the second battle of the Great War. During the night and morning of 25-26 August 1914 a savage and chaotic fight took place through and around the town of Landrecies. His rapid action at Landrecies, just 20 metres from the Germans was crucial in saving the battalion from heavy machine-gun and rifle fire, which enabled the Coldstreamers to hold their positions during the hours of darkness.

He rejoined the Police Force in 1924 and served for a further 10 years, before leaving to work a small holding in the rural village of Sprotborough, near Doncaster. His death occurred at Sprotborough in January 1964 aged 77. He was survived by his wife Ellen.

Lieutenant Colonel Walter Herbert Young D.S.O
1st Battalion East Yorkshire Regiment 1914

Walter Herbert Young was born in Kent in 1870. A distinguished career soldier, he first joined the 15th Foot East Yorkshire Regiment in 1889. A decade later he served as a captain (during the Boer War) with the 2nd Battalion East Yorkshire Regiment and was promoted to the rank of major in 1908. Although not a local man by birth, Walter Herbert Young was well known and respected in Hull and Beverley for his years of service with the East Yorkshire Regiment. Both Young and Richard Erle Benson had served together for almost 25 years by the time of the First World War. After the death of Lieutenant Colonel Richard Erle Benson, Walter Herbert Young, the senior major took over temporary command of the 1st East Yorks in October 1914. By December 1914, of the original 27 officers who had arrived at the Aisne in September, thirteen had been killed and Major Young was just one of six still serving at the front four months into the War. This amounted to casualties of 78 per cent killed, wounded and missing.

Young was awarded the D.S.O in February 1915. He was one of just 37 officers from the East Yorkshire Regiment to win the Distinguished Service Order during the course of the war. He was gazetted to Brevet Lieutenant Colonel in February 1915, before being posted to the 2nd East Yorks in May 1915, just after the Second Battle of Ypres. He later became the C.O of the 2nd Battalion Green Howards in July 1915. Walter Herbert Young was Mentioned in Dispatches three times in 1915, 1916, and 1917. He had been at the front from September 1914 and survived the entire duration of the war serving as the commanding officer of several Yorkshire Battalions.

Young was living in Devon when he applied for his medals in 1921. In December 1931, he sat for his photographic portrait at the National Portrait Gallery in London, then aged 61. The portrait helps to convey the dignity and quiet strength of a man who had done and witnessed so much. Having served his country in two wars, Boer War veteran, "Old Contemptible" and survivor Walter Herbert Young passed away in 1940, aged 70, as the nation had just become involved in another great conflict.

Lieutenant Colonel Walter Herbert Young, in civilian life in 1931, aged 61

Pte 9881 Sam Langrick
1st East Yorkshire Regiment

Sam Langrick, from Wellsted Street in Hull, was working as a joiner in 1914. As a Reservist, he was called back to the 1st Battalion East Yorkshire Regiment on 5th August 1914. After surviving the battles of the Aisne and Armentières, Pte Sam Langrick wrote home to his mother in December 1914, asking if she could send him some cigarettes and football papers. Despite the heavy casualties amongst the 1st Battalion during 1914 and throughout the rest of the conflict, Sam Langrick survived, finishing the war as a sergeant. He lived into old age dying in Hull in 1969 at the age of 82.

The 1914 Star (Mons Star)

The huge casualties amongst the men of 1914 helped to ensure that the 1914 Star or (Mons Star as it is often called, after the first major engagement of the war), was the first campaign medal of the war to be struck in 1917. It was issued to the men of the BEF and the Royal Flying Corps, who served in Belgium and France between August 5th and 22nd November 1914. There were less than 230,000 awarded to the men who would later become known as the Old Contemtibles. This particular 1914 Star was issued to 7444 Private L. Edmondson 4th Dragoon Guards who was involved in one of the first actions of the war on Saturday 22nd August near Mons.

Conclusion

At the outbreak of War, the BEF's role was to support the much larger French Army, who were still wearing uniforms more in keeping with the Napoleonic era. After pursuing the Allied armies to within 40 miles of Paris, the German advance was checked at the Marne. The Retreat from Mons on the 24th August, (or the Great Retreat, as it is also known), lasted 10 days and only ended when Joffre ordered the French Army to halt on the 3rd September and begin an offensive three days later. When a gap in the German lines opened up it was quickly exploited by the French and the BEF, which precipitated a tactical withdrawal by the German Army to the River Aisne where they would dig the first trenches of the war along the high ground above the Aisne. By preventing the fall of Paris and ensuring that the war would continue, the French Army suffered over a quarter of a million casualties, a third of them dead. German losses were over 250,000 and their retreat to the formidable Aisne heights resulted in the abandonment of the Schlieffen plan. This ensured Sir John French and the BEF were not evacuated back to England just a month into the war.

With deadlock at the Aisne in September, the onset of trench warfare and the subsequent stalemate saw massive casualties amongst the old Regular army. The heavy losses in 1914, when known, came as a huge shock to the British public, who had been brought up on the invincibility of the British Empire and had been accustomed to nothing more than the deaths of one or two local professional soldiers that may have occurred during the Boer War. After just two months of war, over 20,000 casualties exceeded those incurred in over two and a half years of conflict during the South African War. By the 1st November, Prime Minister Asquith had to inform the House of Commons that British casualties had reached 58,000 for the three months of the war. Despite the great offensives of 1916-17 the stalemate that had developed during September 1914 would remain in place for most of the duration of the conflict and it was not until the final six months of the war that open warfare began once again, after the Spring Offensive of 1918.

Over 50 per cent of the men serving at the front in 1914 were made up of Reservists, men who had settled back into civilian life and often started families. Within hours, they had been ordered to leave what were often mundane jobs and their families to go back to the military, some of them years after they had last worn a uniform. British casualties were over 90,000 by the end of 1914, whilst around 225 professional servicemen and merchant seamen from Hull lost their lives. This was just over 3 per cent of the city's total number of deaths sustained during the war. But it was the sacrifice made by these professional soldiers that ensured that the European conflict would continue into a second year, developing into what later became known as the Great War. This allowed the survivors of 1914 (and new men of 1915) to carry on the war. It was crucial that the new and inexperienced armies of the following year were ready and able to fight Germany and her allies in the second year of conflict and as the nation's commitment and losses rose so did Hull's. The men of 1915, the Territorials, Colonials, Kitchener's New Armies, were left to fill the void in the second year of the war, ensuring that the numbers of Hull men at the front would increase significantly into thousands, whilst the city's losses would quadruple to almost a thousand during the second year of the conflict. A Territorial Battalion made up of hundreds of Hull men was at the front in April and was thrown into the line at Ypres just six days after their arrival. Within days, the city had lost several prominent Hull businessmen which included a solicitor from Rollit & Co a firm still in business a century later. Several mill managers, a wealthy ship owner and hundreds of local workers were killed, wounded and missing, in what were the first very heavy losses borne by the city but just the start of many as the war deepened. Four months later the city would be left with more heavy losses amongst the 6th East Yorks at Gallipoli, leaving hundreds of men killed wounded and missing, whilst families were left to make desperate appeals through the local newspapers for information on the fate of their sons, brothers and husbands.

Although initially very successful in persuading large groups of local men to join up en masse, the raising of the new armies and the Pals Brigade ensured for the first time that hundreds of local men would have the reassurance of serving with friends, family and work mates. But it had one very obvious drawback in respect of local casualties, meaning that those serving together could and would die together in large numbers as they entered the war and became involved in major engagements at Ypres, in the Dardanelles, Serre, Arras, and Ludendorff's Spring offensive in 1918 .By 1918 the nation was weary. The war and the public's perception was very different to 1914, when Reservists and regular soldiers confidently embarked for France to support the French and Belgian Armies. The men who took the King's shilling in 1914 did so for a multitude of reasons and it would be naïve to imagine that all enlisted for purely patriotic reasons. A chance to travel for the first time, a possible foreign romance, or to escape a dead end job, or a nagging wife, were all motivations but whatever men's personal reasons were ,they all served and endured equally. It would have been too incredible to contemplate for most of the men at the front in 1914, that the death and destruction that they had witnessed at the Aisne and the First Battle of Ypres could carry on for a further four years. They had been told that they would be home by Christmas but they had not been told which one.

So it was the volunteers of 1914 that ensured that the nation could continue to prosecute the war in the second year of the conflict, after the destruction of much of the old professional British Army. The fact that the nation was able to carry on for 18 months, reliant entirely on volunteers, whilst the other combatants had relied on conscription from August 1914, is testament to the spirit of those men enlisting from Hull and across the country in 1914.

Appendix A

Hull Policemen serving with the Coldstream Guards in August 1914

P.C Charles Baker — Carr Lane Beat
P.C John Blyth — Whitefriagate Beat
P.C John Burton
P.C Herbert Cawkwell [Later Lincolnshire Police Force]
P.C Herbert Dearing
P.C P. Hill
P.C Edmund Hilliard
P.C Harold Lyons
P.C Timothy Oliver
P.C Frederick Charles Ware

Numbers serving with the Hull Police Force in 1899

Chief Constable	1
Deputy Chief Constable	1
Superintendents	3
Inspectors	7
Sergeants	32
Detective Officers	11
Constables	223

Appendix B

Hull men serving with the Coldstream Guards in 1914

KIA Killed in Action		DOW Died of Wounds	MD Medically Discharged
Name	Rank	Service	Remarks
Anderson, A	Pte 4093		
Atkinson, Albert	Pte 7329	wounded at the Aisne 1914	MD 31.5.16
Bailey, Arthur	Pte 9703		KIA 28.10.14
Baker, Charles	Pte 10200	Hull P.C lost two fingers	
Barley, William	Pte 5736	Wounded at Ypres	
Barlow, William H.	Pte 12519		KIA 25.2.15
Beneyworth, Frank	Pte 3574		DOW 16.11.14
Bilton, Joseph	Pte 6030	Reservist	KIA 16.9.14
Blackburn, Edward	Pte 12548		KIA 12.3.15
Blackburn, Walter	Pte 5871	Reservist, Hull Postman	
Blanchard, Philip	Pte 11466		DOW 2.2.15
Blyth, John	Pte 6479	Reservist, Hull P.C	
Booker, John	Pte 8732		KIA 25.10.14
Brown, H.S	Pte 9585		
Burton, John	Pte 16682	Reservist, Hull P.C	
Cade, Bob	Cpl		
Cawkwell, Herbert	Pte 5129	Reservist, Hull P.C wounded at Ypres	
Chipchase, Charles	Pte 4333		KIA 5.11.14
Codd, H	Pte 8066	Wounded at Ypres	MD 12.10.18
Cook, Harry	Pte 8621	lost a finger at the Aisne	MD 3.9.15
Corbally, John	Pte 10652	Transferred to Royal Engineers	
Cox, James	Pte 3868		KIA 23.10.14
Crawforth, Samuel	Pte		
Curwen, Wilton	Pte 10287		DOW 28.10.14
Dearing, Herbert	L/Cpl 8503		MD 11.10.17
Dixon, Edmund	Pte 15188		KIA 15.9.16
Escreet, Albert	Pte 5874		DOW 18.11.14
Escritt, Charles	Pte 10077	Enlisted in 1913	MD 14.9.15
Elton, Andrew	Pte 10419		KIA 14.9.14
Fairfield, Joseph	Pte 9801		
Gardiner, James R	Sgt 8613	Shot through the wrist at the Aisne	
Gorman, Andrew	L/Cpl 10714		KIA 29.10.14
Gould, Wilfred	Pte 12549		KIA 14.3.15
Grant, Timothy	Pte 2285	Wounded trying to save his cousin	
Haldenby, Albert	Pte 7317	Reservist	KIA 28.9.14
Haldenby, Arthur R.	L/Cpl 8408	2nd Battalion	
Harrison, George	Pte	Wounded at the Aisne	
Harrison, William	Pte	2nd Battalion	
Harding, Harold	Pte 924	2nd Battalion	DOW 3.11.14
Hart, C.H.	Pte 7890	3rd Battalion Transferred to M.G .Guards	
Hill, P	L/Cpl	Reservist, Hull P.C 1st Battalion	
Hilliard, Edmund	Pte 4291	Reservist Hull P.C	MD 1917
Hobson, John William	Pte 10291	Taken Prisoner returned 27.2.19	
Instone, Leonard F.	Pte 10128	Hull School swimming champion	KIA 1.5.15
Kemp, Walter	Pte 10103	Injured in the foot at Soupir Farm	
Kirk, Randall	Pte 8716		DOW 27.9.14

Name	Rank/Number	Notes	Fate
Kirk, Arthur	L/Cpl 5949		
Kirk, William	Pte 15894		KIA 15.9.16
Knowles, J.A	Pte 10252		DOW 13.10.14
Laver, William	Pte 10143	Wounded at the Aisne 1914	
Lockwood, Mark	Pte 7346	Wounded at the Marne	DOW 9.9.14
Lynch, James R.	L/Cpl 5692	Head wounds evacuated to Dunkirk,	DOW 14.10.15
Lyons, F. Harold	Pte 8481	Reservist, Hull P.C	
Marshall, Frederick	Sgt 843	Posted missing January 1915	KIA 25.1.15
Mearn, William P.	Pte		1st Battalion
McNeill, Albert H	Pte 10627		KIA 29.10.14
Newman, John	Pte	2nd Battalion	
Nicholson, John	Pte 10347		KIA 19.11.14
Oliver, Timothy	Pte 3170	Reservist, Hull P.C	KIA 25.12.14
Perkins, George	Pte 8985	Taken Prisoner 1914	
Raper, Albert	Pte 9398	Reservist, N.E.R signalman	KIA 26.12.14
Real, W	Pte	3rd Battalion	
Redhead, P Solomy	Pte 7904		KIA 29.10.14
Redhill, P	Pte	1st Battalion	KIA 29.10.14
Rispin, Fred	Pte 6027	1st Battalion	KIA 29.10.14
Robinson, Leonard	Pte 4796/11463	December draft 1914 awarded DCM in 1916	
Senior, John	Pte 9770/	Awarded the DCM 16.1.15	
Shakesby, George	Pte 7512		KIA 1.2.15
Simpson, W.L	Pte		
Spires, George	Pte	Reckitts employee	KIA 22.12.14
Smith, J.A	Pte	Promoted L/Cpl 1914	
Smith, B.H	Pte	1st Battalion wounded January 1915	
Smith, Raymond	L/Cpl 11542		DOW 29.12.17
Smith, Thomas	Pte 10229		DOW 16.9.15
Stainforth, George	Pte 10230		
Stamp, C.A	Pte 5346	Posted to M.G. Guards 1.2.17	
Stokes, Albert	Pte 11450		DOW 22.12.14
Teasdale, Albert	Pte 6107	Reservist	DOW 9.9.14
Teasdale, Samuel	Pte 20199	2nd Battalion	DOW 31.7.17
Tessyman, Harold	Pte 7800	Posted to M.G Guards 5.5.15	
Thackeray, Lionel E	Pte 11054		KIA 25.1.15
Thorley, Reginald	Pte 10598		
Thorrold, Frederick L.	Pte 10348	Shot through the arm at Soupir	MD 29.4.15
Waltham, William E	Pte 6423		DOW 9.11.14
Warden, Sidney	Pte 8072	shot in the foot at Soupir	
Warcup, Bernard	L/Sgt 7934	Prisoner of War	
Ward, Fred	Pte	2nd Battalion	
Ware, Frederick C.	Pte 3010	Reservist, Hull P.C	
Wells, Frank	Pte 10603		KIA 22.12.14
Wells, Robert	Pte 5297		KIA 25.8.14
Wells, Richmond	Pte 11449	Awarded the Military Medal	
West, John	L/Cpl 8333	Taken prisoner Ypres 1914	
Whiteley, Jack	Pte 7238	1st Battalion wounded at the Aisne	
Withers, Arthur P	Pte 12892		KIA 20.3.15

This is not a complete list of all Hull men serving with the three Battalions of the Coldstream Guards August-December 1914 as no such records exist and I apologise to those families who are not listed here. The local men recorded here have been uncovered by searching local newspapers, military service records, Regimental War Diaries, the 1901,1911 census's and the records of the Commonwealth War Graves Commission.

Appendix C

Officers serving with the 1st Battalion East Yorkshire Regiment in September 1914

Lt Colonel Richard Erle Benson	DOW 27.9.14
Major Walter Herbert Young D.S.O	
Major W.E Campion	KIA 28.10.14
Captain Wood RAMC -Medical Officer	
Captain D.F Anderson D.S.O	
Captain Eric .Priestly Edwards,	KIA 20.9.14
Captain Peter B. Maxwell,	DOW 24.9.14
Captain B.W Bogle,	
Captain B. Lawrence,	KIA 26.10.14
Captain A.H Wilson,	KIA 18.10.14
Captain F. Hind,	DOW 29.10.14
Lieutenant N.V. Blacker,	
Lieutenant Basil Stewart C. Hutchinson,	KIA 20.9.14
Lieutenant Leadley-Brown,	
Lieutenant F.H Sasse,	
Lieutenant H.S. Cosens,	KIA 27.10.14
Lieutenant V.E Inglefield,	
Lieutenant J. A Markham,	
2nd Lieutenant P. Clutterbuck,	KIA 20.10.14
2nd Lieutenant A. W Meller	KIA 20.9.14
2nd Lieutenant J.A. Hartcup	
2nd lieutenant T.M Robson	
2nd Lieutenant R.T Scott,	
2nd Lieutenant Mark Robinson Pease,	KIA 20.10.14
Lieutenant & Q.M Hon. John Horrocks, Died Heart Failure 23.10.15	
2nd Lieutenant T.R Bottomley,	KIA 22.9.14
2nd Lieutenant G.R. Smallwood,	

Appendix D

Hull Officers serving with the 1/4th East Yorkshire Regiment in April-May 1915

Lieutenant Colonel George Hubert Shaw		KIA 24.4.15
Major Carl Eric Theilmann		KIA 24.4.15
Major Arthur Easton	Promoted Lt Colonel 1915	
Major Herman Joseph Gosschalk		
Captain Cyril Easton M.C		KIA 23.4.17
Captain Bede Farrell		KIA 24.4.15
Captain Cecil J. Ingleby	Promoted Major	
Captain Thomas James Morrill	Promoted Major	
Captain Bernard Marshall Sharp	Shrapnel wounds	
Captain Charles Harland Judge	Wounded 1915	DOW 17.5.15
Captain Cecil Moorhouse Slack M.C	Taken Prisoner April 1918	
Captain P. Robson		
Lieutenant Harry Dales	Wounded 1915	
Lieutenant James Rishworth		KIA 3.5.15
Lieutenant Frank Norman Saxelbye		DOW 11.5.15
Lieutenant Frank Grindell	Buried by a shell April 1915	
Lieutenant Adrian Farrell	Brother of Bede	DOW 23.8.16
2nd Lieutenant Sidney Hannaford Hellyer	Arm blown off	DOW 8.5.15
2nd Lieutenant N A. Thorp	Wounded 1915	

Appendix E

Hull men killed serving with 1/4th East Yorkshire Regiment Second Battle of Ypres April 22 May 25

Ainley, Charles Pte 1638		KIA 1.5.15
Alcock, George A. Pte 1803		KIA 3.5.15
Amos, Archibald Pte 2350		KIA 24.5.15
Bayford, Albert Pte 2887		DOW 17.5.15
Boardman, Frank Pte 1253		KIA 4.5.15
Bowden, John R Pte 2535		KIA 24.4.15
Boyes, Harold Sgt 1480	D Company	DOW 31.5.15
Blyth, Charles Pte 1189		KIA 3.5.15
Brady, Walter Pte 2250		KIA 3.5.15
Branton, Alfred Pte 2160		KIA 24.4.15
Broadley, Thomas Pte 3050		DOW 26.4.15
Burley, Arthur G. Pte 1135		KIA 2.5.15
Carr, Stanley Edwin Pte 1431		DOW 29.4.15
Carver, Arthur Pte 2549		KIA 24.4.15
Clarke, Ernest Pte 3330		DOW 5.5.15
Colley, Wilfred Pte 1268		KIA 3.5.15
Crowther, Thomas Pte 2297		KIA 29.4.15
Dalton, Percival Pte 2368		KIA 25.4.15
Davey, James Pte 1593		KIA 24.4.15
Davison, Fred Cpl 1065		KIA 2.5.15
Devine, Thomas Pte 1866		KIA 3.5.15
Everitt, James W. Pte 2748		KIA 28.4.15
Ferrand, Herbert Harold CSM 6	Boer war Veteran	KIA 26.4.15
Gouldthorpe, Alfred Pte 1682		DOW 1.5.15
Hair, Harold Pte 1617		DOW 6.5.15
Hall, Thomas Pte 2471		KIA 24.5.15
Harper, Bernard Pte 1913		KIA 3.5.15
Hathaway, Joseph Pte 1446		KIA 4.5.15
Hearfield, Charles E Pte 2123		KIA 28.4.15
Hebden, Charles A Pte 2477		KIA 4.5.15
Hilton, Arthur Sgt 1062		KIA 3.5.15
Hymas, Ernest Pte 3262		KIA 3.5.15
Isaac, Augustus Pte 2261		KIA 4.5.15
Jackson, John Sgt 1365	Boer War veteran	KIA 3.5.15
James, Edward Cpl 1331		KIA 3.5.15
Jeffery's, Robert Pte 1716		KIA 2.5.15
Jewitt, Robert W. Pte 2980		KIA 4.5.15

Jollands, James Leo Cpl 1434		KIA 2.5.15
Jones, Maurice James Pte 2649		KIA 24.5.15
Jones, Wilfred Robert Pte 3306		DOW 4.5.15
Kidd, Thomas Pte 1828		KIA 3.5.15
Kitching, Alfred Pte 1904		KIA 24.4.15
Martin, Charles Pte 1822		KIA 3.5.15
Mason, George E Pte 1301		KIA 3.5.15
Matsell, George Pte 2378		DOW 3.5.15
Mitchell, Lawrence Sgt 733		KIA 3.5.15
Newlove, Alfred L. Pte 1293		KIA 2.5.15
Norton, William Pte 2364	Shrapnel wounds	DOW 3.5.15
Oliver, John H Pte 1760		KIA 3.5.15
Paton, George Pte 2422		KIA 2.5.15
Robinson, Harry E. Cpl 76		KIA 26.5.15
Scott, Robert Pte 2238		KIA 3.5.15
Simpson, Ernest Pte 1680		DOW 21.5.15
Smethurst, Walter Pte 2725		KIA 3.5.15
Smith, Joseph Helm Pte 2852		KIA 3.5.15
Snee, William Pte 1687		DOW 6.5.15
Steele, Mathew J. L/Cpl 2476		KIA 26.5.15
Stockdale, John Robert Pte 1628		KIA 24.4.15
Storey, Charles Pte 2914		KIA 3.5.15
Thomas, Alfred Pte 2371		KIA 3.5.15
Tummon, Robert Pte 1214		KIA 25.4.15
Wade, Arthur Pte 2370		KIA 1.5.15
Walters, Milward H. Pte 3140		KIA 28.4.15
Watson, Arthur Pte 1588		KIA 2.5.15
Webster, George Henry Pte 1647		KIA 2.5.15
Wharam, William Pte 1964		KIA 3.5.15
Wrigglesworth, Albert Pte 2498		DOW 30.4.15
Wright, Percy Pte 2665		KIA 3.5.15

This may not be a complete list of all those Hull men killed serving with the 4th East Yorks in April-May 25th during the Second Battle of Ypres 1915. To those families not recorded here, I apologise and hope that they can take great pride in their relations actions in such a crucial battle.

Appendix F

Battalion Commanders killed, whilst serving with the East Yorkshire Regiment 1914-15

Of the seven battalion commanders holding the rank of Lieutenant Colonel killed, whilst serving with the East Yorkshire Regiment three had already lost their lives by August 1915.

Lieutenant Colonel Richard Erle Benson
1st Battalion East Yorkshire Regiment

Richard Erle Benson was the first battalion commander of the East Yorkshire Regiment to lose his life during the war. He succumbed to his wounds at the Base Hospital at St Nazaire on 27th September 1914 after being injured in his first action of the war whilst leading from the front. Born into a distinguished military family in 1862, Benson was a career soldier, with his service beginning in 1884. He served in South Africa during the Boer War when he was briefly attached to the East Surreys. He became the commanding officer of the 1st East Yorkshire Regiment in August 1911, and after his death in 1914, his body was returned to England for a family burial, whilst his wife placed a memorial plaque to his memory in Beverley Minster just a short distance from where the cenotaph to the East Yorkshire Regiment stands.

Located in Beverley Minister memorial to Lieutenant Colonel. Richard Erle Benson

Lieutenant Colonel George Hubert Shaw, 4th Battalion East Yorkshire Regiment

Although many of the Battalion Commanders of the East Yorkshire Regiment were not local men, George Hubert Shaw was, born in Hull in 1864. He combined a successful career as a malting and barley merchant with his part time military service with the Volunteer Battalion East Yorkshire Regiment which began in 1883. In 1911 he became the C.O of the 1/4th East Yorks and volunteered for overseas service in 1914. The Hull Territorial Battalion contained more Hull officers than almost any other battalion from the East Yorkshire Regiment in 1915. Shaw was one of three senior officers all Hull men killed when leading the Territorial Battalion in their first battle of the war at St Julien Second Battle of Ypres. His death left a widow and four grown up children one of them a serving officer in France. Francis Leslie, the 21 year old son of George Hubert Shaw, was killed in September 1916 serving with the Canadians.

Lieutenant Colonel Henry Glanville Allen Moore, 6th Battalion East Yorkshire Regiment

Moore was the son of a Dorset vicar and was born in Nottingham in 1865 and enlisted in the ranks of the Grenadier guards in 1886. He was gazetted 2nd Lieutenant in 1891 and served in the Egyptian Campaign of 1898. He later transferred to the East Yorkshire Regiment in 1908. At the outbreak of war he was promoted to Lieutenant Colonel and was instrumental in training the recently formed 6th East Yorkshire Regiment part of Kitchener's New Armies. His death at Gallipoli a year into the war was an act of murder a war crime which left a widow and two daughters in England.

Captain Osborn Cecil Wilkinson, 2nd Battalion East Yorkshire Regiment

Osborn Cecil Wilkinson was not a battalion commander nor was he born in Hull but he is another man remembered by his wife on the walls of Beverley Minster. He was one of two officers killed by the same shell and one of five officers and 73 other ranks from the 2nd Battalion East Yorkshire Regiment to lose their lives during February 1915.

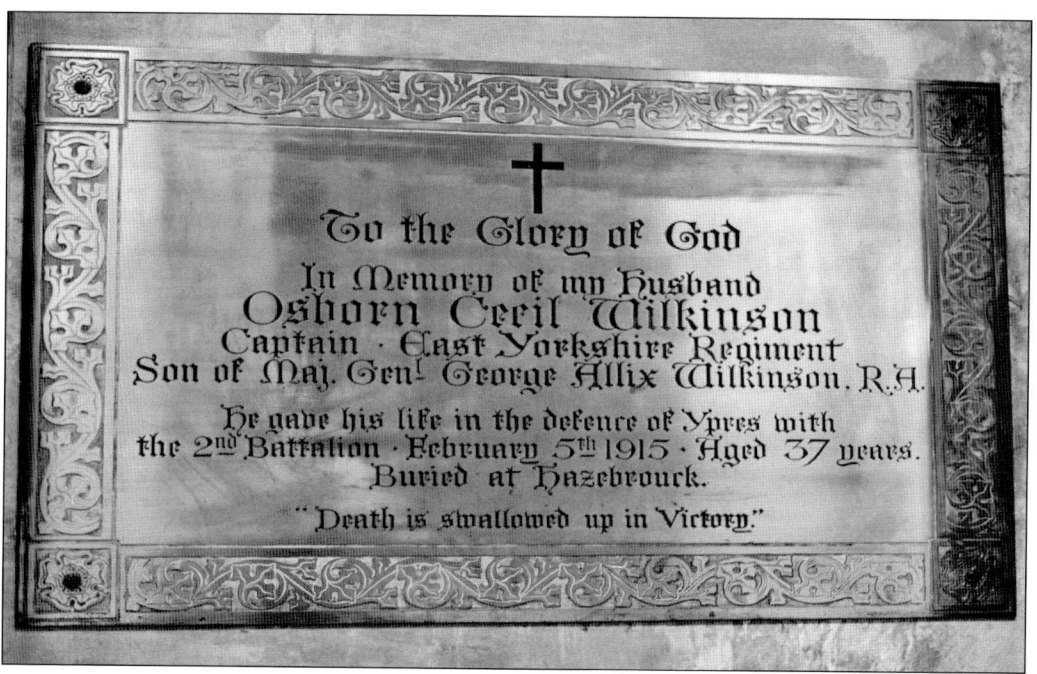

Memorial plaque to Captain. Osborn Cecil Wilkinson, Beverley Minster

Key World and Local Events of 1915

19th January	First Zeppelin raid, civilians killed at Great Yarmouth and Kings Lynn
22nd April	Germans use poison gas for the first time on the Western Front
22nd April	Beginning of the Second Battle of Ypres 22 April- 25 May
23-24 April	2nd East Yorks and 4th East Yorks enter the Second Battle of Ypres
25th April	First Gallipoli landings at Cape Helles
3rd May	Heavy bombardment of 4th East Yorks Trenches, 22 Hull men killed
7th May	Sinking of Lusitania by a German U-Boat resulting in American deaths
25th May	Shell crisis results in Asquith having to form a coalition government
6th June	First Zeppelin raid on Hull resulting in 24 deaths
6th August	New landings allied offensive at Suvla and Anzac Cove
9th August	6th East Yorks attack Tekke Tepe, over 50 Hull casualties
21-22 August	6th East Yorks attack "W" Hill more Hull casualties
25th September	The British Army use poison gas for the first time at the Battle of Loos
12th October	British nurse Edith Cavell is executed by a German firing squad
14th October	Bulgaria declares war on Serbia
26th October	2nd East Yorks embark for Salonika
10th December	Sir Douglas Haig replaces Sir John French as Commander in-Chief BEF
17th December	The Derby Scheme fails the Military Service Act becomes law in 1916

Primary Sources
Regimental War Diaries

The War Diary of 1st Battalion Coldstream Guards August-December 1914 WO 95 /1263/1

The War Diary of 2nd Battalion Coldstream Guards August-December 1914 WO 95/1342/2

The War Diary of 3rd Battalion Coldstream Guards August-December 1914 WO 95/1343/3

The War Diary of 1st Battalion East Yorkshire Regiment August 1914-January 1915 WO 95/1618/1

The War Diary of 2nd Battalion East Yorkshire Regiment August 1914-December 1916 WO 95/2834/1

The War Diary of 1/4th Battalion East Yorkshire Regiment August 1914-December 1915 WO 95/2834/1

The War Diary of 6th Battalion East Yorkshire Regiment (Pioneers) July-December 1915 WO 95/4298/

The Snapper February 1922, Lieutenant Colonel Walter Herbert Young, September-October 1914

Newspapers

The Hull Daily Mail 1914, 1915, 1916, 1917, 1918,

The Hull Daily News 1914, 1915, 1916, 1917, 1918,

The Hull and East Lincolnshire Times 1915

Hull and East Yorkshire Times 1914

The Times 1914, 1915

The London Gazette 1889, 1895, 1914, 1915, 1916, 1917,

Directories/Others

The Mann Collection Vol 1 Hull Daily Mail 1914-15

Kelly's Directory of Hull and its neighbourhood 1899

Hull Peace Souvenir 1919

Online

Ancestry Co. UK Draft, Enlistment, and Service

Ancestry Census Returns, 1881,1891,1901,1911,

Ancestry De Ruvigny's Roll of Honour, 1914-1919 Bede Farrell Vol 1

The Commonwealth War Graves Commission http://www.cwgc.org

The Gallipoli Association http://www.gallipoli-association.org

The Long, Long Tail the British Army in the Great War of 1914-18 the East Yorkshire Regiment in the Great War

http://www.1914-1918.net/eastyorks.htm

British Merchant and Fishing vessels lost August-December 1914

http://wwwnaval-history-net/WW1NavyBritishBVLgm [Accessed October 2014]

Hull Trawler http://www.trawler.net

Bibliography

Ascoli David, *The Mons Star The British Expeditionary Force* (London; Harrap Ltd 1981)

Barthorp Michael, *Blood-Red Desert Sand the British Invasion of Egypt and the Sudan 1882-1898* (London: Cassel & Co 1984)

Barnes B.S, *This Righteous War*, (Netherwood Press: 1990)

Barnes B.S, *Known To the Night* (Hull: Sentinel Press 2002)

Barnes B.S, *Known Unto God a History of Beverley and the Great War 1914-1924* (Sentinel Press 2013)

Chapman Peter, *Grimsby's Own the story of the Chums* (Beverley: Hutton Press Ltd: 1991)

Erickson J, *Gallipoli and the Middle East 1914-1918* (London: Amber Books Ltd 2008)

Fosten D.S.V & Manon R.J *The British Army 1914-18* (London: Osprey Military 1991)

Gillett Edward and MacMahon A. Kenneth *A History of Hull* (Hull: Oxford University Press 1980)

Gliddon Gerald, 1914 *VCs of the First World War* (Gloucestershire: Alan Sutton Publishing Ltd 1994)

Holmes Richard, *The Western Front* (London: BBC Worldwide Ltd 1999)

Kendall Paul, *Aisne 1914 the Dawn of Trench warfare* (Gloucestershire: The History Press 2012)

Kimberley Stephen, *Humberside in the First World War* (Hull; Local History Archives 1988)

Laffin John, *Damn the Dardanelles the Agony of Gallipolli* (Great Britain: Alan Sutton Publishing 1989)

Macdonald Lynn *1915* (London: Headline Publishing 1993)

Salter J. A CB *Economic and Social History of the World War* (Oxford: Claredon Press 1921)

Simkins Peter, *Kitchener's Army the Raising of the New Armies 1914-16* (Barnsley: Pen & Sword 2007)

Sumner Ian, *The Wolds Wagoners the story of the Special Reserve* (Sledmere Estate: 2000)

Taylor A.J.P *The Struggle For Mastery in Europe 1848-1918* (Oxford: Oxford University Press 1971)

Taylor James, *Ellermans a Wealth of Shipping* (London: Wilton House Gentry 1976)

Van Emden Richard, *Prisoners of the Kaiser The Last POWs of the Great War* (Barnsley: Pen & Sword 2004)

Walker R.W, *Recipients of the Distinguished Conduct Medal 1914-1920* (Birmingham; Galata Coins Ltd 1981)

Wyrall Everard, *The East Yorkshire Regiment in the Great War 1914-18* (London: Harrison & Sons Ltd 1928)

Index

A
Adams, James 99
Ainley, Charles 128
Airy, Richard 99
Amos, Archibald 83, 128
Armstrong, William Herbert
Addyman, Oscar James 67
Anderson, A 128
Anthony, Reginald, 54,55,56
Aske, Robert, 71
Atkinson, William, 61
Atkinson, William Fewlass, 95

B
Bailey, Arthur, 124
Baker, Charles, 28,123,124
Barley, William, 124
Barlow, William, 124
Barnard, Charles, 58
Barney, James, 42
Barrass, Alfred Leonard, 42
Bayford, Albert, 128
Beneyworth, Frank, 124
Benson, Richard Erle, 35,36,39,43, 126,130
Bilton, Joseph, 7,10,17,18,124,
Blackburn, Edward, 124
Blackburn, Walter, 17,124
Blacker, N.V, 1
Blanchard, Philip, 124
Blyth, Charles, 82,128
Blyth, John, 28,123,124,
Boardman, Frank, 128
Boddy, Thomas, 39,40
Bogle, B.W, 126
Bond, John, 40
Booker, John, 24,124
Bowden, John, 128
Boyd, Douglas, 50,53, 107
Brady, Walter, 128
Brain, John Charlie, 41
Branton, Alfred, 128
Broadley, Thomas, 128
Brown, H.S, 124
Brumpton, Ernest, 61
Burley, Arthur, 128
Burton, John, 29,124

C
Cade, Bob, 124
Campion, W.E, 126
Carr, Stanley Edwin, 128
Cawkwell, Herbert, 123, 124
Chipchase, Charles, 124
Clarke, Ernest, 128
Clarke, John Louis Justin, 103
Clutterbuck, P, 126
Codd, H, 124
Cook, Harry, 10,11, 124
Colley, Wilfred, 124,
Corbally, John, 124
Cosens, H.S, 124
Cowper, Malcolm Gordon, 96
Cox, James, 124
Crawforth, Samuel, 124
Crowther, Thomas, 128
Curwen, Wilton, 24, 124

D
Dalton, Percival, 128
Davey, James, 128
Davison, Fred, 128
Dearing, Charles, 128
Dearing Herbert, 7, 29, 123, 124
Devine, Thomas, 82, 128
Dinsdale, George, 106, 107
Dixon, Edmund, 124
Dobson, Frederick William, 22, 23

E
Easton, Arthur, 74, 83, 126
Easton Cyril, 126
Edwards, Eric, Priestly, 38
Elton, Andrew Ernest, X, 1, 16, 18, 124,
Escreet, Albert, 124,
Escritt, Charles, 124
Estridge, Cecil, Loraine, 101
Everatt, Charles, 99

F
Fagg, William, 59, 60
Fairfield, Joseph, 124
Farmery, Louis, 40
Farrell, Adrian, 127
Farrell Bede, 74, 83, 127
Ferrand, Herbert Harold, 128
Franklin, Arthur, 61

G

Gardiner, James, 29, 124
Gardiner, Edgar, 39
Gorman, Andrew, 24, 124
Gosschalk, Herman Joseph, 74, 127
Gould, Andrew, 124
Gouldthorpe, Alfred, 1, 128
Grant, Timothy, 7, 124
Grindell, Frank, 78, 127

H

Haldenby, Albert, 17, 22, 23, 124
Haldenby, Arthur, 22, 124
Hair, Harold, 124
Hall, Herbert, 39
Hall, Thomas, 128
Hart, C, 41, 124,
Harding, Harold, 124
Harrison, George, 10, 21, 124
Harrison, William, 21, 124
Harper, Bernard, 128
Hastings, Charles, 61
Hathaway, Joseph, 128
Hearfield, Charles, 128
Hebden, Charles, 128
Hellyer, Charles Peabody, 80
Hellyer, Charles, 80
Hellyer, Jane Victoria Hannaford, 75
Hellyer, Sidney, 74, 75, 77, 78, 79, 80, 126
Hill, P, 29, 123, 124
Hilliard, Edmund, 29,
Hilton Arthur, 82, 128
Hind, F, 126
Hobson, John William, 33, 124
Hodges, Charles, 40
Horrocks, Hon. John, 103, 104, 126
Howard, John, 40
Hurd, Thomas, 80
Hutchinson, Basil Thomas, 126
Hymas, Ernest, 128

I

Ingleby, Cecil, 72, 127
Inglefield V.E, 126
Instone, Leonard Frederick, X, 1, 10, 26, 27, 124,
Isaac, Augustus, 128

J

Jackson, John, 73, 76, 82, 128
Jackson, Thomas, 58
Jackson, William, 54
James, Edward, 128
Jeffrey, Robert, 128
Jenkins, John, 53, 54
Jewitt, Robert, 128
Jollands, James Leo, 128
Jones, Maurice James, 129
Jones, Wilfred Robert, 129
Joyce Frederick, 99
Judge, Charles Harland, 82, 127

K

Kemp, Walter, 17
Kennedy, James,
Kidd, Thomas, 82
Kirk, Arthur, 125
Kirk, Randall, 17, 124
Kirk, William, 125
Kitching, Alfred, 129
Knaggs, Francis, 39
Knowles, John Albert, 10, 23, 125

L

Langric, Sam, 42, 120
Laver, William, 125
Lockwood Mark, 13, 17, 125
Lyons, Harold Frederick, 17, 28, 123, 125

M

Markham, J.A, 126
Marshall, Frederick, 29, 125
Martin, Charles, 129
Mason, George, 129,
Matsell, George, 129,
Maxwell, Peter, 126
McNeil, Albert, 125
Mearn, William, 125
Mee, George Hamilton, 98
Mileham, Frederick, XI
Mitchell, Lawrence, 82, 129
Moore, Henry Glanville Allen, 88, 90, 92, 93, 94, 131,
Morrold, Walter, 99
Morton, Joseph, 39
Murray, Stanley, 83

N

Newman, John, 125
Nicholson Henry, 99
Nicholson, John, Charles, 25, 26, 125
Norton, William, 39, 82

O

Ohlson, Eric, 108
Oliver, John, 129
Oliver, Timothy, 29, 125

P

Parrott, Harry Rands, 40
Paton, George, 129
Payne, Henry Drummond, 68
Pease, Mark Robinson, 43, 126
Perkins George, 125,
Pougher, William, 39
Poulson, Hilmer, 39

Q

Quaid, Charles Edward, 39

R

Raper, Albert, 29, 31, 125
Real, W, 125
Redhead, Percy Solomy, 24, 125
Redhill, P, 125
Risdale, R, 83,
Rispin, Fred, 24, 25, 125
Rishworth, James, 74, 82, 127
Robinson, Harry, 126,
Robinson, Leonard, 125
Robson, Thomas, 12
Robson, T.M, 126

S

Sanderson, Harry, 54
Sassee, F.W, 126
Saxelbye, Frank Norman, 83, 126

Scott, Robert, 129
Senior, John, 125
Shakesby George, 125
Sharp, Bernard Marshall, 81, 127
Sharp, James, X
Shaw, George Hubert, 72, 73, 78, 127
Simpson, Ernest, 129
Simpson, W.L, 125
Slack, Cecil Moorhouse, 32, 116, 127
Smallwood, G.R, 126
Smethurst, Walter, 129
Smith, B.H, 125
Smith-Dorrien, Horrace, 12, 68
Smith, J.A, 125
Smith, Joseph Helm, 129
Smith, Merton Beckwith, 23, 24, 110
Smith, Raymond, 125
Smith, Thomas, 125
Snee, William, 129
Stainforth, George, 125
Stamp, C.A, 125
Steele, Mathew, 126
Stockdale, John Robert, 129
Stokes, Albert, 125
Storey, Charles, 129

T

Taylor, Ben, 62, 63
Teasdale, Albert, 13, 14, 17, 18, 125
Teasdale, Albert Anthony, 14
Teasdale, Marguerrita, 14
Teasdale, Sam, 14, 125,
Tessyman, Harold, 125
Thackeray, Lionel, 125
Theilmann, Carl Eric, 73, 74, 78, 127
Thomas, Alfred, 129
Thompson, Herbert Ernest, 95,
Thorley, Reginald, 125
Thorp, N.A, 127
Thorpe, George Robert, 61
Thorrold, Frederick Livingston, 16, 111, 125
Tock, Stanley, 88, 89, 99, 114, 115,
Tock, Wilfred Wilson, 88
Traynor, William Bernard, 5, 6
Tummon, 129

W

Wade, Arthur, 129
Walker, John 99
Walker, Robert Henry, 59
Waltham, William, 125
Walters, Milward, 129
Warcup, Bernard, 10, 125
Ward, Fred, 125
Warden, Sidney, 7, 21, 125
Ware, Frederick Charles, 7, 27, 113, 125,
Watson, Arthur, 129
Webster, George Henry, 129
Wells, Robert, 12, 13, 18, 29, 125
Welsh, Joseph, 39
West, John, 32, 33, 125
Whitely, Jack, XI, 125
Withers, P, 125
Wilkinson, Osborn Cecil, 67, 132
Wilkinson, Arthur Henry, 126
Willey, George William, 54
Wing, Thomas, 95
Wood, John Edward, 99
Wood, Miss (VAD) 49
Wollaston, Frederick William, 63, 112
Wrigglesworth, Albert, 129
Wright, Percy, 129
Wyatt, George Frederick, 12, 22, 117

Y

Young, Walter Herbert, 39, 43, 44, 118, 119, 126